Staff Training & Development

MW01482256

About This Book

Why Is This Topic Important

This book was written because training professionals and department managers are often assigned the task of coming up with a training plan and corresponding budget. They often don't know how to perform the needs assessment necessary to come up with numbers they can defend.

What Can You Achieve with This Book

The purpose of this book is to walk readers step-by-step through the process of developing a training plan and budget. The book comes complete with questions to ask, a case example to review, and templates to fill in. It tells the reader how to use the information gathered in one step as a building block for the next.

By reading this book and completing the templates, readers can develop a training plan and budget that are linked to strategic business objectives.

How Is This Book Organized

This book is organized around a ten-step process for generating a realistic training budget. Each step is described in detail and includes a case study and sample templates. Blank copies of the templates are included at the back of the book as well as on the accompanying CD-ROM.

About Pfeiffer

Pfeiffer serves the professional development and hands-on resource needs of training and human resource practitioners and gives them products to do their jobs better. We deliver proven ideas and solutions from experts in HR development and HR management, and we offer effective and customizable tools to improve workplace performance. From novice to seasoned professional, Pfeiffer is the source you can trust to make yourself and your organization more successful.

Essential Knowledge   Pfeiffer produces insightful, practical, and comprehensive materials on topics that matter the most to training and HR professionals. Our Essential Knowledge resources translate the expertise of seasoned professionals into practical, how-to guidance on critical workplace issues and problems. These resources are supported by case studies, worksheets, and job aids and are frequently supplemented with CD-ROMs, websites, and other means of making the content easier to read, understand, and use.

Essential Tools   Pfeiffer's Essential Tools resources save time and expense by offering proven, ready-to-use materials—including exercises, activities, games, instruments, and assessments—for use during a training or team-learning event. These resources are frequently offered in looseleaf or CD-ROM format to facilitate copying and customization of the material.

Pfeiffer also recognizes the remarkable power of new technologies in expanding the reach and effectiveness of training. While e-hype has often created whizbang solutions in search of a problem, we are dedicated to bringing convenience and enhancements to proven training solutions. All our e-tools comply with rigorous functionality standards. The most appropriate technology wrapped around essential content yields the perfect solution for today's on-the-go trainers and human resource professionals.

Essential resources for training and HR professionals

Training Budgets Step-by-Step

A Complete Guide to Planning and Budgeting Strategically-Aligned Training

Diane C. Valenti

Pfeiffer

A Wiley Imprint
www.pfeiffer.com

Published by Pfeiffer
An Imprint of Wiley.
989 Market Street, San Francisco, CA 94103-1741   www.pfeiffer.com

For additional copies/bulk purchases of this book in the U.S. please contact 800-274-4434.

Pfeiffer books and products are available through most bookstores. To contact Pfeiffer directly call our Customer Care Department within the U.S. at 800-274-4434, outside the U.S. at 317-572-3985 or fax 317-572-4002 or visit www.pfeiffer.com.

Pfeiffer also publishes its books in a variety of electronic formats. Some content that appears in print may not be available in electronic books.

Printed in the United States of America

ISBN: 0-7879-6889-7

Library of Congress Cataloging-in-Publication Data
Valenti, Diane C.
    Training budgets step-by-step: a complete guide to planning and budgeting strategically-aligned training/Diane C. Valenti.
        p. cm.
Includes bibliographical references and index.
    ISBN 0-7879-6889-7 (alk. paper)
  1. Employees—Training of—Planning. 2. Employees—Training of—Finance. I. Title: Complete guide to planning and budgeting strategically-aligned training. II. Title.
    HF5549.5.T7V2   2004
    658.3'12404—dc21

                                2003011161

Acquiring Editor: Matthew Davis
Director of Development: Kathleen Dolan Davies
Developmental Editor: Susan Rachmeler
Editor: Rebecca Taff
Senior Production Editor: Dawn Kilgore

Manufacturing Supervisor: Bill Matherly
Interior Design: Bruce Lundquist
Cover Design: Michael Cook
Illustrations: Lotus Art

Printed in the United States of America
Printing   10   9   8   7   6   5   4   3   2   1

Contents

To my husband, Steve, who always believed in me.

Acknowledgments

I GREATLY APPRECIATE MY REVIEWERS, who provided feedback before this book was even a book. Thank you to Pat Shuman, Tony Harter, Jana Humphreys, and especially to Nancy Magsig, who came up with the idea of including templates.

I want to thank my clients, who gave me a chance to work on large curriculum projects that provided me with a chance to figure out how to plan and budget training and development projects. And I especially want to thank Lori Serrano, my very first client.

Thanks also to my editor, Pat Tshirhart-Spangler, who made sure my manuscript was word perfect before I sent it to publishers for consideration. And thanks to Georgia Graham, who made sure the manuscript looked great.

I also want to thank my editors at Pfeiffer. Your recommendations took this book to a whole different level.

Last, I want to acknowledge and thank my friends and family for their varied contributions.

- To Steve, my husband, who always believed in me.

- To my parents, Ed and Joan Valenti, for their support in encouraging me to write and teach as I was growing up. Their encouragement eventually helped me launch a career.

- To my friends and family, who have helped me create balance (and sanity!) in my life over the years. Thank you Laura and Matt Bartelli, Lynne Barnett, Steve and Erika Valenti, Perry Valenti, Nina Maslo, Sandy and Larry Willig, Ken, Martine, Maxine, and Zakk Clark, Jennifer Selby, Linda Fairchild, Chuck and Ako Willen, Shannon Bresnahan, Susan and Frank Chaney, Diana and Herman Van Elburg, Dave Obler, Lisa Fraser, Larry Tokar, Sandy McFall, Bill Gambrell, Chuck and Eileen Mooring, Lisa Fraser, Gordon Hauschild, Bruce Honig (whose book comes out just a few months before mine), Izabel Loinaz, Ann Allison-Marsh, Marti Conger, and Ryan Yee.

- To my grandmother, Edith Clark, for providing a model of strength, dignity, and resilience. And to my grandfather, Roy Clark, who showed me what it took to run a business.

- To Jill Welch, who unknowingly steered me into this field after college.

- To Jill Lublin at Promising Promotion for her help in getting this book noticed.

- To my many associates who have helped me make Applied Learning Solutions a truly virtual company. Every time we've worked together, I've learned something.

- And, finally, to Leon, Tribble, and Spike, my furry friends in charge of employee morale.

Introduction

Purpose

In most cases, the goal of training is to solve problems, achieve goals, and resolve issues to support your organization in achieving its strategic objectives. This guide walks you step-by-step through the planning process, so that you can develop a training plan and budget that supports your organization's efforts to achieve its objectives. It comes complete with questions to ask, a running case study, and templates to fill in.

In some situations, though, training alone will not be enough to solve the problem, achieve the goal, or resolve the issue. This guide also allows you to determine whether training is the appropriate response.

How to Use These Materials

This guide consists of three parts:

- Instructions on how to perform each step
- A case study that illustrates the process
- Blank templates for your use

To get the most from this guide, review the example of the finished plan shown in Template 14 beginning on page 108. Then return to the beginning and read the instructions and review the intermediary examples to see the output of each step. Italicized text shows how the output of previous steps is used in the current step. With the exception of the first step where all information is new, shaded text shows new information that results from the current step.

When you are ready to create your own training plan and budget, you can photocopy the blank templates in the Appendix or print them out from the accompanying CD-ROM. Then follow the instructions to complete them.

One caveat—if you do not have the time or resources to complete each step, do what you can. Also feel free to divide the work involved among several people.

How This Book Is Organized

The flowchart in the following figure provides an overview of the process of creating a training plan and budget. A brief description of each step follows the flowchart.

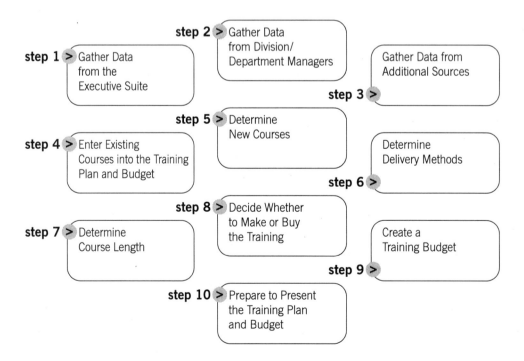

Step 1: In this step, you'll meet with the executive team to learn about problems that need to be solved and goals that need to be achieved for the organization to be successful.

Step 2: In this step, you'll meet with division/department managers to learn more about the role these divisions/departments will play in solving the problems and achieving the goals that the executive team has identified. You'll also learn about any issues that each division/department is facing that are preventing it from meeting its goals.

Step 3: In this step, you'll identify existing training offered through the training department and independently within specific divisions/departments. You'll also determine whether or not training, or training alone, is the appropriate response to solving the problems, achieving the goals, and resolving the issues that have been identified.

Step 4: In this step, you'll determine which existing courses to include in this year's training plan.

Step 5: In this step, you'll determine what new courses you'll need to add to the training curriculum to solve the problems, achieve the goals, and resolve the issues that have been identified.

Step 6: In this step, you'll determine how new courses will be delivered. For example, should Interviewing 101 be delivered in the classroom or over the company's intranet?

Step 7: In this step, you'll make an educated guess on the length of each new course.

Step 8: In this step, you'll decide whether to make or buy new courses.

Step 9: In this step, you'll cost out the training you need to buy or develop.

Step 10: In this step, you'll prepare to present the first draft of the training plan and budget to your supervisor for approval.

Gather Data from the Executive Suite

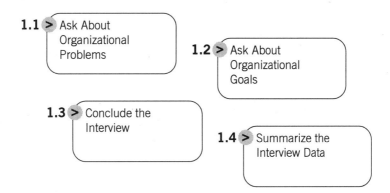

1.1 > Ask About Organizational Problems

1.2 > Ask About Organizational Goals

1.3 > Conclude the Interview

1.4 > Summarize the Interview Data

Purpose

To begin the process, you'll need to interview the executive team to learn about problems that need to be solved and goals that need to be achieved for the organization to be successful. This will give you the information you need to ensure that the training plan you create is aligned with organizational objectives.

Templates

You'll need the following templates to complete this step:

- Executive Interview Summary—Organizational Problems (Template 1)
- Executive Interview Summary—Problem Worksheet (Template 2)
- Executive Interview Summary—Organizational Goals (Template 3)
- Executive Interview Summary—Goal Worksheet (Template 4)

Ask About Organizational Problems (1.1)

Interview members of the executive team one at a time. Use the questions below to ask about organizational problems.

1. What critical problems is the organization facing?
2. How would you prioritize these problems? Please begin with the one most critical to organizational success and go from there.

For each problem, ask the following questions:

1. What is the problem? Please describe the problem in detail.
2. What operational results will indicate the problem has been solved?
3. Why is solving the problem critical to achieving organizational success?
4. Which divisions or departments will be involved in solving each problem?
5. What will the employees in these divisions or departments need to do or do differently to solve each problem? How are employees performing today? How will they need to perform to solve the problem?
6. What, if anything, will employees in these divisions or departments need to learn so that they can solve each problem?
7. Besides employee performance, what other factors contribute to each problem?

8. What changes do you plan to make to address these contributing factors (for example, introduce a new system, change job responsibilities, and so forth)?

9. Which divisions or departments will be impacted by these changes?

10. What, if anything, will employees in these divisions or departments need to learn as a result of these changes (for example, if a new system is introduced, employees will need to learn how to use it)?

Ask About Organizational Goals (1.2)

Use the questions below to ask about organizational goals.

1. What are the organization's goals for the next business year?

2. How would you prioritize these goals? Please begin with the one most critical to organizational success and go from there.

Then, for each goal, ask the following questions:

1. What is the goal? Please describe the goal in detail.

2. What operational results will indicate the goal has been achieved?

3. Why is achieving the goal critical to achieving organizational success?

4. Which divisions or departments will be involved in achieving each goal?

5. What will the employees in these divisions or departments need to do or do differently to achieve each goal? How are employees performing today? How will they need to perform to achieve the goal?

6. What, if anything, will employees in these divisions or departments need to learn so that they can achieve each goal?

7. Besides employee performance, what other barriers get in the way of achieving each goal?

8. What changes do you plan to make to overcome these barriers (for example, introduce a new system, change job responsibilities, and so on)?

9. Which divisions or departments will be impacted by these changes?

10. What, if anything, will employees need to learn as a result of these changes (for example, if a new system is introduced, employees will need to learn how to use it)?

Conclude the Interview (1.3)

Conclude the interview by asking, "Is there anything I did not ask that I should have?" Then thank the executive for his or her time.

Explain that you will provide a copy of your notes for review to ensure that you captured the information accurately. This also gives the executive the opportunity to add anything he or she may have forgotten during the interview.

Summarize the Interview Data (1.4)

After you have completed the interviews, you'll need to validate the interview data. Complete an Executive Interview Summary—Organizational Problems form (Template 1) listing all the problems and an Executive Interview Summary—Organizational Goals form (Template 3) listing all the goals each executive identified. Next, document the details of each problem on an Executive Interview Summary—Problem Worksheet (Template 2) and of each goal on an Executive Interview Summary—Goal Worksheet (Template 4). Then send the completed worksheets to the executive for review. You may also want to follow up with a phone call to make sure that you captured the information accurately and to find out whether the executive has anything to add.

Then you'll need to summarize the data for all interviews on one set of templates. This means you'll need one final set of Templates 1 through 4 that pull together all of the problems and goals previously identified.

If executives noted different strategies for accomplishing goals or are planning different changes to solve a problem, make sure to include them all on this version of the templates. You can then present your findings to the executive team or a steering committee so that members can reach consensus on these discrepancies. This will allow you to ensure that the training plan you create supports organizational objectives.

Each of the ten steps in the process will be illustrated by a running case study with sample templates. The first part of the case follows.

Case Study

All American Insurance is a personal lines property and casualty insurance company, with headquarters in San Jose, California. It provides auto and homeowners insurance through its burgeoning network of branch offices, which are primarily concentrated in the Western states of California, New Mexico, and Utah.

Adjusters working out of a central call center in Sacramento, with the aid of a network of contracted auto repair shops and general contractors, investigate and resolve simple, minor auto and homeowners claims. If the claim is complex or major, adjusters in the call center refer it to the branch office closest to the insured's location. Adjusters located in these branch offices investigate and resolve all complex and major claims.

"It's that time of year again," J.P. Clark, director of training for All American, thinks, as she gathers up her notebook and heads out to meet with the VP of operations. Time to prepare the training budget for the next fiscal year. It is still early in September, but with fiscal year-end looming on January 31st, J.P. feels the pressure to start moving.

She is scheduled to spend an hour meeting with Barbara Anderson, VP of Operations, to discuss company challenges and goals for next year that might require the Training Department's support. She has already met with the vice presidents of Fraud Prevention, Litigation, Risk Management, and Sales.

The vice president of sales was not happy with how far the sales of homeowners insurance was lagging behind that of auto insurance. He was also adamant that something had to be done about the high turnover of salespeople in the branch offices. And all mentioned the need to develop bench strength among senior managers to create a pool from which to identify and promote future executives.

"It'll be interesting to hear what Barbara has to say," J.P. muses. A lot of changes took place last year in All American's Claims Division.

The company recently opened the call center in Sacramento and staffed adjuster positions with relatively inexperienced adjusters. While they only handle fairly simple, small dollar claims,

J.P. has heard that many are struggling with the basics of what to do when they are assigned a claim.

And, while call center supervisors are very experienced, they are spread thin. Often twenty or more adjusters will report to a single supervisor. So supervisors' ability to help newly minted adjusters is limited by their lack of availability.

J.P. knocks lightly on the door frame of Barbara's open office door, and Barbara beckons her in.

Once J.P. completes her meeting with Barbara, she lists all of the challenges Barbara mentioned on the Organizational Problems Summary Sheet (see Template 1) and all of the goals on the Organizational Goals Summary Sheet (see Template 3). She also captures the details of each problem on a separate Problem Worksheet (see Template 2) and of each goal on a separate Goal Worksheet (see Template 4). Then she emails all this information to Barbara to make sure she's captured Barbara's thoughts accurately. Then she follows up with a phone call to see if there is anything Barbara wants to change or add.

After she has completed this process for all the executives, J.P. will summarize all problems on a single Organizational Problem Summary Sheet and all goals on a single Organizational Goals Summary Sheet. She'll also summarize the data for each problem on a separate Problem Worksheet and for each goal on a separate Goal Worksheet.

For example, since several executives mentioned the need to develop bench strength among senior managers to prepare them for executive positions, J.P. will summarize all their comments about this problem on a single Problem Worksheet.

If J.P. finds discrepancies in the strategies or changes executives plan to implement to address a specific problem or accomplish a specific goal, she'll ask to be included on the agenda for the weekly top team meeting. This will give her a chance to clarify these discrepancies with executives so that she can ensure the training plan she creates supports the steps they plan to take to achieve organizational objectives.

Template 1

Executive Interview Summary—Organizational Problems

Name > Barbara Anderson

Title > Vice President/Operations

Date > 09/01/03

Prioritize the problems based on how critical they are to organizational success.

Organizational Problems

High Priority > Adjusters are not complying with the Department of Insurance (DOI) regulations. ◄─── We will follow this problem through the example.

Adjusters are not adjusting third-party claims. They are just paying the bills.

Turnover among insurance salespeople is too high.

Medium Priority >

Low Priority >

Template 2
Executive Interview Summary—Problem Worksheet

Name > Barbara Anderson

Title > Vice President/Operations

Date > 09/01/03

Complete a Problem Worksheet for each problem.

Problem > What is the problem?

Adjusters are not complying with DOI regulations.

_____

Operational Results > What operational results will indicate that the problem has been solved?

When supervisors performed quality checks of adjusters' files, they found problems with approximately 70 percent of the files.

100 percent of all files should be in compliance with DOI regulations.

_____

Priority > Why is solving the problem critical to achieving organizational success?

All American Insurance risks fines for noncompliance.

Template 2 *(continued, p. 2)*

Executive Interview Summary—Problem Worksheet

Division/Departments Involved in Solving the Problem	Actual Performance Today	Performance Required to Solve the Problem	Anticipated Learning Needs
> Claims.	Adjusters seem to be oblivious about DOI regulations.	Adjusters should monitor regulations to ensure their files remain in compliance.	What DOI regulations are.

Executive Interview Summary—Problem Worksheet

Factors Contributing to the Problem	Planned Changes to Address Factors	Divisions/Departments Impacted by Changes	Anticipated Learning Needs
> Adjusters are very busy and often don't remember DOI regulations, even if they know what they are.	Add pop-up box reminders to the claims resolution software that will be triggered based on the date the claim was opened and the steps the adjuster has taken to resolve the claim.	Claims.	None.

Template 3

Executive Interview Summary—Organizational Goals

Name > Barbara Anderson

Title > Vice President/Operations

Date > 09/01/03

Prioritize the goals based on how critical they are to organizational success.

Organizational Goals

High Priority > Improve customer service by reducing
the time it takes to resolve a claim.

We will follow this
goal through the
example.

Medium Priority > Increase sales of homeowners insurance.

Develop bench strength among senior level managers
to ensure there is an adequate pool of employees from
which to draw executives.

Low Priority >

Template 4

Executive Interview Summary—Goal Worksheet

Name > Barbara Anderson

Title > Vice President/Operations

Date > 09/01/03

Complete a Goal Worksheet for each goal.

Goal > What is the goal?

Improve customer service by reducing the time it takes to resolve a claim.

Operational Results > What operational results will indicate the goal has been achieved?

Reduce claim resolution time from 30 to 25 days for 75 percent of all claims.

Priority > Why is achieving the goal critical to achieving organizational success?

Recent customer satisfaction surveys indicate that the timely resolution of claims is a big issue for our policyholders.

Executive Interview Summary—Goal Worksheet

Division/Departments Involved in Achieving the Goal	Actual Performance Today	Performance Required to Achieve the Goal	Anticipated Learning Needs
> Claims.	We have recently hired many new adjusters who are unfamiliar with the claim resolution process. They must wait for input from supervisor to determine what to do. They also must be walked step-by-step through the process by a supervisor or more experienced peer.	Adjusters need to resolve claims, except in unusual cases (for example, there is a question of whether coverage applies), with minimal supervision.	What the steps are to resolve each type of claim.

Template 4 *(continued, p. 3)*

Executive Interview Summary—Goal Worksheet

Barriers to Achieving the Goal	Planned Changes to Overcome Barriers	Divisions/Departments Impacted by Changes	Anticipated Learning Needs
> The ratio of employees to supervisor is too high. Supervisors are stretched too thin to even be able to provide timely assistance to adjusters facing unusual coverage issues.	Hire experienced supervisors from competitors. Promote from within when possible.	Claims. Human Resources.	Claims—how to conduct behavioral interviews.
> There is no way to assign more complex claims to experienced adjusters.	Implement a workload-balancing application to assign claims based on complexity and current workload.	Information Technology. Claims.	Claims—how to use the workload-balancing application to assign claims to adjusters.

Gather Data from Division/Department Managers

2.1 > Prepare for the Interview

2.2 > Share Organizational Problems

2.3 > Ask About Organizational Problems

2.4 > Share Organizational Goals

2.5 > Ask About Organizational Goals

2.6 > Ask About Division/Department Issues

2.7 > Ask About Existing Training

2.8 > Conclude the Interview

2.9 > Summarize the Interview Data

2.10 > Share Data with Executives

Purpose

You'll need to interview division/department managers to get more detail about the top-down findings you gleaned from the executive interviews. The purpose of these interviews is threefold:

- To validate (confirm) what employees in each division/department need to learn so they can solve problems and achieve goals identified by the executive team

- To gather information on other issues that are impacting each division/department

- To find out about existing training employees are attending

Templates

You'll need the following templates to complete this step:

- Division/Department Manager—Organizational Problems (Template 5)
- Division/Department Manager—Problem Summary (Template 6)
- Division/Department Manager—Problem Worksheet (Template 7)
- Division/Department Manager—Organizational Goals (Template 8)
- Division/Department Manager—Goal Summary (Template 9)
- Division/Department Manager—Goal Worksheet (Template 10)
- Division/Department Manager—Issues (Template 11)
- Division/Department Manager—Issue Worksheet (Template 12)
- Existing Training Worksheet (Template 13)

Prepare for the Interview (2.1)

If the executive team identified a division/department as being involved in solving a problem or achieving a goal, you'll need to summarize the data collected during the executive team interviews.

Problems:

1. Create a list of problems the division/department will be involved in solving. See the example of Template 5, Division/Department Manager—Organizational Problems on page 30. This information can be gleaned from Template 1, as appropriate for each division/department.

2. For each problem, summarize information that pertains to this division/department from the executive team interviews. (Multiple divisions/departments may be involved in solving a particular problem.) See the example of Template 6, Division/Department Manager—Problem Summary on pages 31 and 32. Much of this information can be taken from Template 2, as appropriate for each division/department.

3. Send this information to the manager for review before the interview.

Goals:

1. Create a list of goals the division/department will be involved in achieving. See the example of Template 8, Division/Department Manager—Organizational Goals on page 35. This information can be taken from Template 3, as appropriate for each division/department.

2. For each goal, summarize information that pertains to this division/department from the executive team interviews. (Multiple divisions/departments may be involved in achieving a particular goal.) See the example of Template 9, Division/Department Manager—Goal Summary on pages 36 and 37. This information can be gleaned from Template 4, as appropriate for each division/department.

3. Send this information to the manager for review before the interview.

If the executive team did not identify this division/department as being involved in solving a problem or achieving a goal, you may begin the interview with a discussion of issues facing this division/department. See the example of Template 11, Division/Department Manager—Issues on page 40.

You may wish to ask the manager beforehand to prepare information on the following topics:

- Issues the division/department is facing

- Existing training division/department employees are attending

Share Organizational Problems (2.2)

Share with the manager the organizational problems the executive team believes this division/department will be involved in solving. Then share the following information:

- A description of each problem

- The operational results that will indicate the problem has been solved

- Why solving the problem is important to the organization

- What executives believe employees in this division/department need to do or do differently to solve the problem

- What executives believe employees need to learn to solve the problem

- What other factors executives feel are contributing to the problem

- What changes executives plan to make to address these factors

- What executives believe employees in this division/department will need to learn as a result of these changes

Ask About Organizational Problems (2.3)

Give the manager a chance to discuss each problem by asking these questions:

1. What positions within your division/department will be involved in solving this problem? Find out specific job titles, number of employees, and location for each position mentioned.

2. How are employees performing today?

3. In your opinion, how will they need to perform to solve the problem?

4. What, if anything, will employees in these positions need to learn to solve the problem?

5. In your opinion, what other factors contribute to the problem?

6. What additional changes may need to be made to address these factors?

7. Which positions within your division/department will be impacted by these changes? Find out specific job titles, number of employees, and location for each position mentioned.

8. What, if anything, will employees in these positions need to learn as a result of these changes?

Share Organizational Goals (2.4)

Share the organizational goals the executive team believes this division/department will be involved in achieving. Then share the following information:

- A description of each goal

- The operational results that will indicate that the goal has been achieved

- Why achieving the goal is important to the organization

- What executives believe employees in this division/department need to do or do differently to achieve the goal

- What executives believe employees need to learn to achieve the goal

- What barriers executives feel are getting in the way of achieving the goal

- What changes executives plan to make to overcome these barriers

- What executives believe employees in this division/department will need to learn as a result of these changes

Ask About Organizational Goals (2.5)

Give the manager a chance to discuss each goal by asking these questions:

1. What positions within your division/department will be involved in achieving this goal? Find out specific job titles, number of employees, and location for each position mentioned.

2. How are employees performing today?

3. In your opinion, how will they need to perform to achieve the goal?

4. What, if anything, will employees in these positions need to learn to achieve the goal?

5. In your opinion, what barriers get in the way of achieving the goal?

6. What additional changes may need to be made to overcome these barriers?

7. Which positions within your division/department will be impacted by these changes? Find out specific job titles, number of employees, and location for each position mentioned.

8. What, if anything, will employees in these positions need to learn as a result of these changes?

Ask About Division/Department Issues (2.6)

Now you'll shift your focus to issues specific to this division/department. Find out what issues this division/department is facing and how critical they are to organizational success. For each issue, ask the following questions:

1. What is the issue? Please describe it in detail.

2. What do you believe is the cause of this issue?

3. What are the results? What difficulty is this issue causing?

4. What operational results will indicate this issue has been resolved?

5. Can this issue be linked to a problem or goal the executive team identified? If so, how?

If employee performance is identified as a possible cause of an issue, ask the following questions:

1. What positions will be involved in resolving this issue? Find out specific job titles, number of employees, and location for each position mentioned.

2. What does actual performance look like today? What does desired performance look like?

3. What, if anything, do employees need to learn to perform as desired?

4. Besides employee performance, what barriers do you think are getting in the way of resolving this issue?

5. What changes do you plan to make to overcome these barriers?

6. Which positions will be impacted by these changes? Find out specific job titles, number of employees, and location for each position mentioned.

7. What, if anything, will employees in these positions need to learn as a result of these changes?

Ask About Existing Training (2.7)

Finally, inquire about any existing training. For example, employees in the claims division of an insurance company may all take a course on Department of Insurance (DOI) regulations.

Once the manager has given you a list of existing training courses, ask the following questions:

1. Is this list of courses current? What, if any, courses are obsolete? What, if any, courses will we need to add? Modify the list as needed.

2. Who must attend each course? How large is this group? Where are they located?

3. Are any of these courses mandatory? For which audiences?

4. How is each course currently delivered (classroom, WBT, or other means)?

5. What is the length of each course?

6. How much does it cost to deliver each course?

7. How often is each course delivered (once a quarter, once a year, or whatever the interval)?

8. Are these courses up-to-date, or do we need to revise them?

9. How extensive do you think these revisions will be? What must be changed?

Conclude the Interview (2.8)

Conclude the interview by asking, "Is there anything I did not ask that I should have?" Thank the manager for his or her time.

Explain that you will provide a copy of your notes for review to ensure that you captured the information accurately. This also gives the manager the opportunity to add anything he or she may have forgotten during the interview.

Summarize the Interview Data (2.9)

Summarize the interview data on the templates. Then send the completed templates back to the manager to review to make sure you captured the information accurately. You may also want to follow up with a phone call to see whether the manager has anything to add.

See the examples of Templates 7 (pages 33 and 34), 10 (pages 38 and 39), 11 (page 40), 12 (pages 41 through 43), and 13 (page 44).

Share Data with Executives (2.10)

After you've validated the interview data with the manager, you'll need to share any discrepancies with the executive the manager reports to.

Specifically, you'll want to let the executive know about the following:

- Any additional factors contributing to problems (Template 7)

- Any additional changes that need to be made to address factors (Template 7)

- Any additional barriers that are getting in the way of achieving a goal (Template 10)

- Any additional changes that need to be made to overcome barriers (Template 10)

- Issues impacting the division/department whether or not they are directly linked to the organizational problems and goals the executive team identified (Templates 11 and 12)

With the addition of this information from the trenches, the executive team may decide to modify its strategy for achieving organizational objectives. You'll need to follow up to see whether any modifications the executive team makes impact the training plan and budget.

Case Study

Note: As you review the sample templates for this step, remember that italics indicate the output from a previous step and shading indicates new information that results from this step.

J.P. breathes a sigh of relief as she steps out of the top team meeting. She now has a big picture of the problems and goals All American's executives plan to address in the coming year. Next, she'll need to dig a little deeper to see what, if any, supporting role training will play.

Once she is back at her desk, J.P. dials Sue Smith, manager of the Claims Division. The fact that, according to executives, adjusters are not complying with Department of Insurance (DOI) regulations is a top-priority problem. It could result in hefty fines being imposed on All American Insurance.

As a matter of fact, the Claims Division is going to be highly involved in solving organizational problems and achieving organizational goals next year, J.P. realizes as she glances down at her notes. It looks like Sue is also on the hook for reducing the time it takes to resolve a claim and for getting her staff to do a better job of investigating and making appropriate payments on third-party claims.

J.P. schedules a meeting with Sue later that week to discuss these issues, as well as to probe for other potential training-related issues Sue is facing. J.P. will also ask about existing training Claims Division employees are already attending.

In the interim, J.P. emails Sue a list of organizational problems and goals the Claims Division will be involved in addressing, along with the corresponding Problem and Goal Worksheets that capture any details she gathered in her executive interviews. In the email message, she also asks Sue to think about other issues Claims is facing and to prepare a list of training courses Claims employees attend.

When J.P. arrives for her meeting with Sue, Sue is on the phone, typing an email message, and eating her lunch simultaneously. "It looks like another busy day in Claims," J.P. thinks. J.P. quietly settles herself in a chair facing Sue's desk. As she finishes her call, Sue dumps one of many stacks of paper on the floor and motions to J.P. to use the now clear section of the desk as a writing surface.

During her discussion with Sue, J.P. learns that adjusters may not know that their files are out of compliance. Apparently, supervisors do not check adjusters' files to make sure they are in compliance, so they cannot point out compliance issues to adjusters. As a result, there are no consequences to adjusters for not meeting DOI regulations.

Plus, according to Sue, existing training on DOI regulations is ineffective. As a result, adjusters may not remember what the DOI regulations are or understand how they apply to the process of resolving a claim.

With Sue's help, J.P. is able to identify the positions (adjusters and their supervisors) that will be involved in solving this problem and what people in these positions will need to learn. [See Templates 5, 6, and 7 for J.P.'s summary of the "problem" portion of the interview.]

According to Sue, ineffective training is also the root cause of adjusters' inability to resolve claims in a timely manner. Apparently, existing training only covers policy terms and conditions and DOI regulations. It does not walk adjusters step-by-step through the process of resolving a claim. [See Templates 8, 9, and 10 for J.P.'s summary of the "goal" portion of the interview.]

In addition, two other problems surface during J.P.'s discussion with Sue. Supervisors lack supervisory skills, and many of the new employees All American is hiring into the adjuster position lack fundamental business etiquette skills. [See Templates 11 and 12 for J.P.'s summary of the "issues" portion of the interview.]

J.P. concludes her interview with Sue by learning what training Claims employees are currently attending. [See Template 13 for J.P.'s summary of the current training situation in Claims.]

After the interview, J.P. quickly types up her interview notes and emails them to Sue to make sure that she captured Sue's thoughts accurately. She then schedules a meeting with Barbara Anderson, VP of operations and Sue's boss, to share what she learned.

When she learns of the additional problems that surfaced during J.P.'s interview with Sue, Barbara makes a note to allocate a greater percentage of next year's budget to training than she had originally planned. Barbara hopes that this additional funding will cover the cost of the supervisory skills and basic business etiquette training it appears is so sorely needed by Claims Division staff.

While Sue tackles defining the potential training needs of the Claims Division, her staff members are meeting with other department and division managers to do the same. They'll compare notes later in the process to see if the needs of different departments or divisions overlap. If they find they do, the Training Department may be able to offer a single course to meet these needs.

Template 5

Division/Department Manager—Organizational Problems

Manager >   Sue Smith

Division >   Claims

Date >   09/01/03

Prioritize the problems this division/department will be involved in solving based on how critical they are to organizational success.

Organizational Problems this Division/Department Will Be Involved in Solving

High Priority >   *Adjusters are not complying with DOI regulations.*

We will follow this problem through the example.

Adjusters are not adjusting third-party claims. They are just paying the bills submitted.

Medium Priority >

Low Priority >

Template 6

Division/Department Manager—Problem Summary

Manager > Sue Smith

Division > Claims

Date > 09/01/03

Summarize the data for each problem identified by the executive team that this division/department will be involved in solving. Include only information that pertains to this division/department. Multiple divisions/departments may be involved in solving a particular problem. Review this information with the division/department manager at the start of the interview. In fact, you may want to send this form before the interview to help the manager prepare.

If the executive team did not identify this division/department as being involved in solving any organizational problems, skip the Problem Summary (Template 6) and Problem Worksheet (Template 7).

Problem > What is the problem?

Adjusters are not complying with DOI regulations.

Operational Results > What operational results will indicate that the problem has been solved?

When supervisors performed a quality check of adjusters' files, they found problems with approximately 70 percent of the files.

100 percent of all files should be in compliance with DOI regulations.

Priority > Why is solving the problem critical to achieving organizational success?

All American Insurance risks fines for noncompliance.

Performance Description > What will employees in this division/department need to do or do differently to solve this problem? How are these employees performing today? How will they need to perform to solve the problem?

Adjusters seem to be oblivious about DOI regulations. Adjusters should monitor regulations to ensure their files remain in compliance.

Template 6 *(continued, p. 2)*

Division/Department Manager—Problem Summary

**Anticipated
Learning Needs** > What, if anything, will employees in this division/department need
to learn so they can solve the problem? (List only anticipated
learning needs for employees in this division/department.)

What DOI regulations are.

Contributing Factors > Besides employee performance, what other factors contribute
to the problem?

*Adjusters are very busy and often don't remember DOI
regulations, even if they know what they are.*

Planned Changes > What changes will be made to address these factors? (List only
changes that will impact this division/department.)

*Add pop-up box reminders to the claims resolution software
that will be triggered based on the date the claim was opened
and the steps the adjuster has taken to resolve the claim.*

**Anticipated
Learning Needs** > What, if anything, will employees in this division/department
need to learn as a result of these changes? (List only anticipated
learning needs for employees in this division/department.)

None.

Template 7
Division/Department Manager—Problem Worksheet

Use the information you gather during your interview with the division/department manager to complete the Problem Worksheet. Include data from executive interviews plus new information this manager provides.

Positions Involved in Solving the Problem (Indicate title, number of employees and location.)	Actual Performance Today	Performance Required to Solve the Problem	Anticipated Learning Needs
> Auto Adjusters, 860. Regional offices.	*Adjusters seem to be oblivious about DOI regulations.*	*Adjusters should monitor regulations to ensure that their files remain in compliance.*	*What DOI regulations are.* How DOI regulations apply to resolving auto claims.
> Auto Claims Supervisors, 43. Regional offices.	Rarely check adjusters' files and provide feedback.	Maintain a schedule to check on adjusters' files to make sure they are in compliance.	How often to check files. What to check. What to look for when checking files. When and how to provide feedback to adjusters.
> Homeowners Adjusters, 400. Regional offices.	*Adjusters seem to be oblivious about DOI regulations.*	*Adjusters should monitor regulations to ensure that their files remain in compliance.*	*What DOI regulations are.* How DOI regulations apply to resolving homeowner's claims.
> Homeowners Claims Supervisors, 20. Regional offices.	Rarely check adjusters' files and provide feedback.	Maintain a schedule to check on adjusters' files to make sure they are in compliance.	How often to check files. What to check. What to look for when checking files. When and how to provide feedback to adjusters.

Division/Department Manager—Problem Worksheet

Factors Contributing to the Problem	Planned Changes to Address Factors	Positions Impacted by Changes (Indicate title, number of employees, and location.)	Anticipated Learning Needs
> Adjusters are very busy and often don't remember DOI regulations, even if they know what they are.	*Add pop-up box reminders to the Claims resolution software. that will be triggered based on the date the claim was opened and the steps the adjuster has taken to resolve the claim*	Auto and Homeowners Adjusters, 1260. Regional offices.	None.
	Create a small laminated poster of DOI regulations adjusters can post on the wall of their cubicles.		None.
> There are currently no consequences to the individual adjuster for having out-of-compliance files.	Include the need to comply with DOI regulations in performance appraisal criteria.	Auto and Homeowners Adjusters, 1260. Regional offices.	What criteria Auto and Homeowners Adjusters will be rated on.
		Claims Supervisors, 63. Regional offices.	None.

Template 8

Division/Department Manager—Organizational Goals

Manager > Sue Smith

Division > Claims

Date > 09/01/03

Prioritize the goals the division/department will be involved in achieving based on how critical they are to organizational success.

Organizational Goals this Division/Department Will Be Involved in Achieving

High Priority > *Improve customer service by reducing the time it takes to resolve a claim.*

> We will follow this goal through the example.

Medium Priority > *Develop bench strength among senior level managers to ensure there is an adequate pool of employees from which to draw executives.*

Low Priority >

Template 9

Division/Department Manager—Goal Summary

Manager > Sue Smith

Division > Claims

Date > 09/01/03

Summarize the data for each goal identified by the executive team that this division/ department will be involved in achieving. Include only information that pertains to this division/department. Multiple divisions/departments may be involved in achieving a particular goal. Review this information with the division/department manager at the start of the interview. In fact, you may want to send this form before the interview to help the manager prepare.

If the executive team did not identify this division/department as being involved in achieving any organizational goals, skip the Goal Summary (Template 9) and Goal Worksheet (Template 10).

Goal > What is the goal?

Improve customer service by reducing the time it takes to resolve a claim.

Operational Results > What operational results will indicate that the goal has been achieved?

Reduce claim resolution time from 30 to 25 days for 75 percent of all claims.

Priority > Why is achieving the goal critical to achieving organizational success?

Recent customer satisfaction surveys indicate that the timely resolution of claims is a big issue for our policyholders.

Performance Description > What will employees in this division/department need to do or do differently to achieve this goal? How are these employees performing today? How will they need to perform to achieve the goal?

We have recently hired many new adjusters who are unfamiliar with the claims resolution process. They must wait for input from a supervisor to determine what to do. They also must be walked step-by-step through the process by a supervisor or more experienced peer.

Adjusters need to resolve claims, except in unusual cases (there is a question of whether coverage applies), with minimal supervision.

Template 9 *(continued, p. 2)*

Division/Department Manager—Goal Summary

**Anticipated
Learning Needs** > What, if anything, will employees in this division/department need to learn so they can solve the problem? (List only anticipated learning needs for employees in this division/department.)

What the steps are to resolve each type of claim.

_____

Contributing Factors > Besides employee performance, what other factors contribute to the problem?

1. *The ratio of employees to supervisors is too high. Supervisors are stretched too thin to even be able to provide timely assistance to adjusters facing unusual coverage issues.*
2. *There is no way to assign more complex claims to experienced adjusters.*

_____

Planned Changes > What changes will be made to address these factors? (List only changes that will impact this division/department.)

1. *Hire experienced supervisors from competitors.
Promote from within when possible.*
2. *Implement a workload-balancing application to assign claims to adjusters based on complexity and current workload.*

_____

**Anticipated
Learning Needs** > What, if anything, will employees in this division/department need to learn as a result of these changes? (List only anticipated learning needs for employees in this division/department.)

1. *How to conduct a behavioral interview.*
2. *How to use the workload-balancing application to assign claims to adjusters.*

Template 10

Division/Department Manager—Goal Worksheet

Use the information you gather during your interview with the division/department manager to complete the Goal Worksheet. Include data from executive interviews plus new information this manager provides.

Positions Involved in Achieving the Goal (Indicate title, number of employees and location.)	Actual Performance Today	Performance Required to Achieve the Goal	Anticipated Learning Needs
> New Auto Adjusters, 460. Regional offices.	*New adjusters must be walked step-by-step through the claims resolution process by supervisors and experienced peers.*	*Adjusters need to resolve claims, except in unusual cases (for example, there is a question of whether coverage applies), with minimal supervision.*	*What the steps are to resolve each type of auto claim.* *How to correctly complete each step. What decisions need to be made during the resolution of a claim. How to make those decisions.*
> New Homeowners Adjusters, 150. Regional offices.			*What the steps are to resolve each type of homeowners claim.* *How to correctly complete each step. What decisions need to be made during the resolution of a claim. How to make those decisions.*

Template 10 *(continued, p. 2)*

Division/Department Manager—Goal Worksheet

Barriers to Achieving the Goal	Planned Changes to Overcome Barriers	Positions Impacted by Changes (Indicate title, number of employees, and location.)	Anticipated Learning Needs
> The ratio of employees to supervisors is too high. Supervisors are stretched too thin to even be able to provide timely assistance to adjusters facing unusual coverage issues.	*Hire experienced supervisors from competitors. Promote from within when possible.*	Claims Managers, 7. Regional offices.	*How to conduct behavioral interviews.*
> There is no way to assign more complex claims to experienced adjusters.	*Implement a workload-balancing application to assign claims based application to assign claims based on complexity and current workload.*	Claims Reporting Hotline Representatives, 1,000. Claims Reporting Center.	*How to use the workload-balancing application to assign claims to adjusters.*
> Existing training only covers DOI regulations and policy terms and conditions.	Develop training to cover the specifics of how to resolve each type of claim.	Claims Trainers, 12. Claims Reporting Center. Headquarters.	How to teach new claims courses.

Template 11

Division/Department Manager—Issues

Manager > Sue Smith

Division > Claims

Date > 09/01/03

Prioritize the issues identified by this division/department manager based on how critical they are to organizational success.

Division/Department Issues

High Priority > Supervisors aren't supervising. They
lack the skills to organize, assign, and
evaluate work and to provide employees
with performance feedback.

We will follow this
problem through
the example.

Medium Priority > Many new employees are inexperienced in the business world
and lack the basics of business etiquette.

Low Priority >

Template 12

Division/Department Manager—Issue Worksheet

Complete an Issue Worksheet for each issue identified by this manager.

Issue > What is the issue?

Supervisors aren't supervising. They lack the skills to organize, assign, and evaluate work and to provide employees with performance feedback.

Cause > What is the cause of the Issue?

Due to organizational growth, All American Insurance has had to promote employees into supervisory positions who have no supervisory experience.

Result > What is the result of this issue? What difficulty is this issue causing?

Employees are disorganized. Work is either falling between the cracks or duplicated. Employees also don't know how well they are performing—what they are doing right, what mistakes they are making, or how to correct those mistakes. Ultimately, this impacts the policyholder's experience. We have started to receive policyholder complaints.

In addition, turnover is up and morale is down. Employees feel overwhelmed because of the lack of supervisory support.

Operational Results > What operational results will indicate that the issue has been resolved?

Decrease policyholder complaints by 20 percent.

Decrease turnover by 5 percent.

The Claims Division is in the middle of collecting data on an employee satisfaction survey. We will be able to set operational goals once the survey score is calculated and Claims determines how much employee satisfaction is based on supervisor support.

Link to Problem or a Goal > Can this issue be linked to a problem or goal the executive team identified? If so, how?

If supervisors are able to organize and assign work effectively, Claims may be able to reduce the amount of time it takes to resolve a claim from 30 days to 25 days.

Division/Department Manager—Issue Worksheet

Positions Involved in Resolving the Issue (Indicate title, number of employees, and location.)	Actual Performance Today	Performance Required to Resolve the Issue	Anticipated Learning Needs
> Claims Managers, 7. Regional offices.	Do not spend time coaching new supervisors.	Provide new claims supervisors with guidance on how to supervise employees and provide feedback on their performance.	How to coach employees.
> Experienced Claims Supervisors, 38. Regional offices.	Do not spend time assisting new claims supervisors.	Partner with new claims supervisors to share supervisory tips and tricks.	How to mentor peers.
> New Claims Supervisors, 25. Regional offices.	Are not supervising employees effectively.	Effectively supervise employees.	How to organize work. How to assign work. How to evaluate work. How to provide feedback.

Template 12 *(continued, p. 3)*

Division/Department Manager—Issue Worksheet

Barriers to Resolving the Issue	Planned Changes to Overcome Barriers	Positions Impacted by Changes (Indicate title, number of employees, and location.)	Anticipated Learning Needs
> Claims managers and experienced claims supervisors are already stretched too thin. They may not have the time to do much peer mentoring.	Hire experienced claims supervisors from competitors.	Claims managers, 7. Regional offices.	How to conduct behavioral interviews.

Template 13

Existing Training Worksheet

Add to this Existing Training Worksheet as you interview each person. Don't forget to include courses that don't fall under any particular division/department, such as New Employee Orientation. Ultimately, this worksheet should contain a comprehensive list of existing training that is being offered throughout the organization.

Course Title	Training Audience (Indicate title, number of employees, and location.)	Mandatory? (Yes or No)	Delivery Method (classroom, WBT, etc.)	Course Length	Cost/Session	Number of Sessions per Year	Up-to-Date? (Yes or No)	Notes
> Introduction to DOI Regulations	New Claims Adjusters, 100. Regional offices.	Yes	WBT	2 hours	Not applicable.	Not applicable.	Yes	No revisions needed at this time.
> Achieving Outstanding Customer Service	New Claims Adjusters and Claims Reporting Hotline Representatives, 250. Regional offices. Claims Reporting Center.	No	Classroom	2 days	$50,000, including instructor fee, instructor and participant travel, and meals.	10	Yes	No revisions needed at this time.

Gather Data from Additional Sources

3.1 > Ask about Existing Inter-Divisional/ Departmental Training

3.2 > Identify Training Needs That Require Further Analysis

3.3 > Determine Whether Training Is Appropriate

3.4 > Note If Training Is Not Appropriate

Purpose

In addition to the executive team and division/department managers, you'll need to talk with others in the organization to gather the data you need to create a training plan and budget. Specifically, you'll need to contact:

- Sponsors of existing inter-divisional/departmental training so you can add the training they offer to the Existing Training Worksheet

- Supervisors and employees so you can determine whether or not training is an appropriate strategy to resolve performance issues

Templates

You'll need the following templates to complete this step:

- Division/Department Manager—Problem Worksheet (Template 7)
- Division/Department Manager—Goal Worksheet (Template 10)
- Division/Department Manager—Issue Worksheet (Template 12)
- Existing Training Worksheet (Template 13)

Ask About Existing Inter-Divisional/Departmental Training (3.1)

You'll need to ask sponsors of existing inter-divisional/departmental training the same questions you asked division/department managers on these topics:

1. Is this list of courses current? What, if any, courses are obsolete? What, if any, courses will we need to add? Modify the list as needed.

2. Who must attend each course? How large is this group? Where are they located?

3. Are any of these courses mandatory? For which audiences?

4. How is each course currently delivered (classroom, WBT, or other means)?

5. What is the length of each course?

6. How much does it cost to deliver each course?

7. How often is each course delivered (once a quarter, once a year, or other time increments)?

8. Are these courses up-to-date, or do we need to revise them?

9. How extensive do you think these revisions will be? What must be changed?

You can then add the information they provide to the Existing Training Worksheet. See Template 13 on pages 50 and 51.

Identify Training Needs That Require Further Analysis (3.2)

At this point you may need to do some additional digging to determine whether the needs identified are truly learning needs. Training will work only if the issue is that employees do not have the knowledge or skills to meet performance expectations.

Review the lists of learning needs you generated for each position on the Problem, Goal, and Issue Worksheets. If you suspect a learning need is really another problem in disguise, you'll need to talk to employees and their supervisors to find out whether the reason employees are not performing as required to solve the problem, achieve the goal, or resolve the issue is because they lack the knowledge and skills needed.

For example, if the use of a legacy system that runs slowly and requires a lot of workarounds hampers employees' ability to meet the production schedule, providing systems training won't help. In contrast, if the company plans to implement a new system to replace the legacy system, employees will need systems training to be able to do their jobs.

Determine Whether Training Is Appropriate (3.3)

Meet with supervisors and employees separately to discuss the learning needs in question. Review the performance required to solve the problem, achieve the goal, or resolve the issue.

Then ask the following questions:

1. What is preventing required performance?

2. What happens when you (or your employees) perform as required?

3. How often are you (or your employees) asked to perform as required?

Listen for possible responses listed in the "If. . ." column in the table below. Refer to the "Then. . ." column to determine whether or not training will close the performance gap.

If. . .	Then. . .
Employees don't know they aren't meeting performance expectations	Set expectations and provide feedback
Employees don't have the resources (time, tools, consistent policies, appropriate authority, and so forth) to meet performance expectations	Make resources available
Employees do not have the knowledge and skills to meet performance expectations	Reassign the work, simplify the job, change recruiting criteria, or provide training
Employees are not rewarded or are inadvertently punished for meeting performance expectations	Change the consequences of performance
Employees are rarely asked to perform the "problem" task	Create a job aid or provide refresher training on a regular basis

If you still feel uncertain that training is the right solution, follow up with on-the-job observations. You may be able to tell by observing if there is a barrier, other than lack of knowledge and skills, that is preventing employees from performing as required. For example, an unstable computer program may be preventing employees from meeting production goals.

Note If Training Is Not Appropriate (3.4)

If training is not appropriate, cross the entry off the Problem, Goal, or Issue Worksheet. Then briefly describe in the "Anticipated Learning Needs" column the cause of the gap between actual and required performance and the recommended intervention. See the example of Template 7 on page 52.

Case Study

J.P. assigns Ken and Rashita, two project managers on her staff, to create a comprehensive list of training that is offered throughout the organization. They are able to pull some of these courses, such as New Employee Orientation and Hiring for Success, from the course catalog the Training Department publishes quarterly.

In other instances, though, they need to meet with division and department heads to identify training sponsored by that particular division or department. For example, Rashita learns that the Fraud Prevention Department sponsors a four-hour course on detecting and reporting suspected fraud every quarter for special investigators working out of headquarters.

As a part of their research into each course, Ken and Rashita identify the target audience, whether the course is mandatory, the delivery method, course length, cost per session, number of sessions per year, and whether the course needs to be updated. [See Template 13 for a summary of Ken and Rashita's work.]

In the meantime, J.P. decides to dig deeper into the issue of adjusters not meeting DOI regulations to find out whether new and improved training will really solve the problem. She schedules a series of interviews with Claims Division supervisors to hear their points of view. And she arranges a couple of focus groups comprised of adjusters who have been with All American for three to nine months. At this point in their tenure with All American, adjusters typically have enough experience handling claims to have at least heard of DOI regulations.

From these sources, J.P. confirms that ineffective training is part of the problem. Other solutions All American plans to implement to resolve this problem, including the creation of a poster of DOI regulations adjusters can hang in their cubicles, won't require training support. [See the partial Template 7 sample for a summary of J.P.'s findings.]

Template 13

Existing Training Worksheet

Add to this Existing Training Worksheet as you interview each person. Don't forget to include courses that don't fall under any particular division/department, such as New Employee Orientation. Ultimately, this worksheet should contain a comprehensive list of existing training that is being offered throughout the organization.

Course Title	Training Audience (Indicate title, number of employees, and location.)	Mandatory? (Yes or No)	Delivery Method (classroom, WBT, etc.)	Course Length	Cost/Session	Number of Sessions per Year	Up-to-Date? (Yes or No)	Notes
> Introduction to DOI Regulations	New Claims Adjusters, 100. Regional offices.	Yes	WBT	2 hours	$10,000 to revise.	Not applicable.	Yes	Revise to make effective.
> Achieving Outstanding Customer Service	New Claims Adjusters and Claims Reporting Hotline Representatives, 250. Regional offices. Claims Reporting Center.	No	Classroom	2 days	$50,000, including instructor fee, instructor and participant travel, and meals.	10	Yes	No revisions needed at this time.
> Insurance Fraud Investigation	Special Investigations, 10. Headquarters.	Yes	Classroom	4 hours	$2,500 for instructor fees.	4	Yes	No revisions needed at this time.
> Managing Performance	New supervisors, 75. Regional offices. Claims Reporting Center. Headquarters.	No	Classroom	1 day	$10,000, including participant travel and meals.	4	Yes	No revisions needed at this time.

Template 13 (continued, p. 2)

Existing Training Worksheet

Add to this Existing Training Worksheet as you interview each person. Don't forget to include courses that don't fall under any particular division/department, such as New Employee Orientation. Ultimately, this worksheet should contain a comprehensive list of existing training that is being offered throughout the organization.

Course Title	Training Audience (Indicate title, number of employees, and location.)	Mandatory? (Yes or No)	Delivery Method (classroom, WBT, etc.)	Course Length	Cost/Session	Number of Sessions per Year	Up-to-Date? (Yes or No)	Notes
> New Employee Orientation	New employees, 400. Regional offices. Claims Reporting Center. Headquarters.	No	WBT	2 hours	Not applicable.	Not applicable.	Yes	No revisions needed at this time
			Classroom	1 day	$5,000, including participant travel and meals.	8		
> Hiring for Success	Managers and supervisors involved in hiring, 80. Regional offices. Claims Reporting Center. Headquarters.	No	Classroom	1 day	$10,000, including participant travel and meals.	4	Yes	No revisions needed at this time
> Avoiding Harassment	New employees, 400. Regional offices. Claims Reporting Center. Headquarters.	Yes	WBT	3 hours	Not applicable.	Not applicable.	Yes	No revisions needed at this time
> Conducting Performance Appraisals	New managers and supervisors, 30. Regional offices. Claims Reporting Center. Headquarters.	No	Classroom	1 day	$5,000, including participant travel and meals.	1	Yes	No revisions needed at this time

Template 7

Division/Department Manager—Problem Worksheet

Factors Contributing to the Problem	Planned Changes to Address Factors	Positions Impacted by Changes (Indicate title, number of employees, and location.)	Anticipated Learning Needs
> Adjusters are very busy and often don't remember DOI regulations, even if they know what they are.	Add pop-up box reminders to the claims resolution software that will be triggered based on the date the claim was opened and the steps the adjuster has taken to resolve the claim	Auto and Homeowners Adjusters, 1,260. Regional offices.	None.
	Create a small laminated poster of DOI regulations adjusters can post on the wall of their cubicles.		None.
> There are currently no consequences to the individual adjuster for having out-of-compliance files.	Include the need to comply with DOI regulations in performance appraisal criteria.	Auto and Homeowners Adjusters, 1260. Regional offices.	~~What criteria Auto and Homeowners Adjusters will be rated on.~~ Not a training need. Can notify claims supervisors and adjusters of this change via a memo from Human Resources and/or an article in the employee newsletter.
		Claims Supervisors, 63. Regional offices.	None.

Enter Existing Courses into the Training Plan and Budget

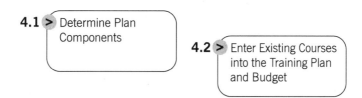

4.1 > Determine Plan
Components

4.2 > Enter Existing Courses
into the Training Plan
and Budget

Purpose

In this step, you'll actually start to build the training plan by adding existing courses you plan to offer again. This is a good time to consider whether the existing training will continue to offer value to the organization. If you can't directly link it to a problem, goal, or issue, you'll need to consider whether you should continue to offer it. In some cases, it may make sense to do so.

For example, it may be difficult to link a course that introduces employees to your organization's business to a problem, goal, or issue. However, this course may be very popular and, at least in part, help maintain employee morale and loyalty to the organization.

Templates

You will need the following templates to complete this step:

- Existing Training Worksheet (Template 13)
- Training Plan and Budget (Template 14)

Determine Plan Components (4.1)

A training plan can become quite large and unwieldy. So you'll need to determine the best way to break it into manageable components. For example, one component might consist of all inter-divisional/departmental courses. You might chunk the rest of the plan by division or department.

Each component of the plan could be further broken down as follows:

- Existing training
- New training that needs to be developed or purchased

Enter Existing Courses into the Training Plan and Budget (4.2)

Start by entering existing training. You may not be able to link existing training directly to a problem, goal, or issue identified during your interviews. If this is the case, make sure to include a brief description of the purpose of the training. See the example of Template 14 on pages 56–58.

This is also a good time to review the purpose of each course to determine whether it is still adding value to the organization.

Use previous years' figures to calculate a realistic budget for the training. Take into account the following figures:

- The number of employees you plan to train this year compared to the number trained in previous years
- The number of sessions you plan to offer this year compared to what was offered in previous years

- The per-session cost of delivery

- The cost of any updates that need to be made to the course

For now, set aside any learning needs that require you to develop or purchase training. We'll cover this in the next step.

Case Study

J.P.'s next step is to meet with Ken and Rashita to start entering existing courses into next year's training plan and budget. Over steaming coffee and donuts, J.P., Ken, and Rashita discuss each existing course on Ken and Rashita's list.

J.P. has prepared for the meeting by summarizing the problems, goals, and issues All American is planning to address next year. After everyone has helped him- or herself to a cup of coffee, J.P. distributes the summary.

J.P. kicks off the meeting by saying, "As we review the list of existing courses, we'll need to make sure each helps All American's employees develop the knowledge or skills they'll need to address at least one of these problems, goals, or issues." She points out that if they can't link a course to a problem, goal, or issue on the summary, they'll need to strongly consider whether it is still adding enough value to continue to include it in next year's training plan.

The team members divide the list of courses among themselves. Each then takes a stab at writing a statement that describes the link between each course and one of the problems, goals, or issues on J.P.'s summary. If they can't easily link the course to a problem, goal, or issue, they add it to a list for later discussion.

Next the team reconvenes and works together to refine their linking statements for each course. J.P. adds the name of the course, the linking statement, and other details, such as delivery method and course length, to the training plan.

The team then turns their attention to the courses they can't easily link to a problem, goal, or issue on the summary. For each of these courses, they determine whether or not the course adds enough value to continue to include it in the training plan.

For example, there is no doubt in anyone's mind that the Fraud Investigation course is a "must-have." Clever con artists are continually coming up with innovative schemes to defraud insurance companies that special investigators need to be briefed on. Similarly, given the need to hire additional supervisors into the call center and deal with the turnover among salespeople in the branch offices, it makes sense to continue to include Hiring for Success on the training plan. [See Template 14 for a summary of the work the team has completed on existing training.]

Template 14

Training Plan and Budget

Existing Inter-Divisional/Departmental Training

Purpose or Link to Problem, Goal, or Issue	Training Audience	Proposed Course	Delivery Method	Course Length	Exists, Develop, or Buy	Budget
> Identify and address harassing behavior.	New employees, 400. Regional offices. Claims Reporting Center. Headquarters.	Avoiding Harassment	WBT	3 hours	Ongoing.	Not applicable.
> Orient new employees to company culture and policies.	New employees, 400. Regional offices. Claims Reporting Center. Headquarters.	New Employee Orientation	WBT	2 hours	Ongoing.	$40,000
			Classroom	1 day		
> Claims Division—need to hire additional supervisors to provide adjusters with the support they need to improve customer service by reducing the time it takes to resolve a claim.*	Managers and supervisors involved in hiring, 80. Regional offices. Claims Reporting Center. Headquarters.	Hiring for Success	Classroom	1 day	Ongoing.	$40,000

*This example only shows links to problems, goals, and issues the Claims Division will be involved in addressing. Your plan would also show links to problems, goals, and issues other division/departments will be involved in addressing.

Template 14 *(continued, p. 2)*

Training Plan and Budget

Existing Inter-Divisional/Departmental Training

Purpose or Link to Problem, Goal, or Issue	Training Audience	Proposed Course	Delivery Method	Course Length	Exists, Develop, or Buy	Budget
> Claims Division—need to provide new supervisors with basic skills. Supervisors lack skills to evaluate work and provide employees with performance feedback.*	New supervisors, 75. Regional offices. Claims Reporting Center. Headquarters.	Managing Performance	Classroom	1 day	Ongoing.	$40,000
	New managers and supervisors, 30. Regional offices. Claims Reporting Center. Headquarters.	Conducting Performance Appraisals	Classroom	1 day	Ongoing.	$5,000

*This example only shows links to problems, goals, and issues the Claims Division will be involved in addressing. Your plan would also show links to problems, goals, and issues other division/departments will be involved in addressing.

Training Plan and Budget

Existing Claims Division Training

Purpose or Link to Problem, Goal, or Issue	Training Audience	Proposed Course	Delivery Method	Course Length	Exists, Develop, or Buy	Budget
> Claims Division—adjusters are not complying with DOI regulations.	New Claims Adjusters, 100. Regional offices.	Introduction to DOI Regulations	WBT	2 hours	Ongoing.	$10,000
> Ensure Investigators are current on the latest insurance fraud schemes.	Special Investigators, 10. Headquarters.	Insurance Fraud Investigation	Classroom	4 hours	Ongoing.	$10,000
> Maintain customer service ratings.	New Claims Adjusters and Claims Reporting Hotline Representatives, 250. Regional offices. Claims Reporting Center.	Achieving Outstanding Customer Service	Classroom	2 hours	Ongoing.	$500,000

Determine New Courses

5.1 > Identify Inter-Divisional/
Departmental
Learning Needs

5.2 > Identify New
Inter-Divisional/
Departmental Courses

5.3 > Identify
Division/Department
Learning Needs

5.4 > Identify New
Division/Department
Courses

5.5 > Add New Courses
to the Training Plan
and Budget

Purpose

Now you'll need to determine what, if any, new courses you'll need to add to the curriculum to address learning needs. Wherever possible, you'll want to identify multiple audiences with the same learning needs who can benefit from a single course. This will help ensure that you get the most for your money.

Templates

You will need the following templates to complete this step:

- Division/Department Manager—Problem Worksheet (Template 7)
- Division/Department Manager—Goal Worksheet (Template 10)
- Division/Department Manager—Issue Worksheet (Template 12)
- Existing Training Worksheet (Template 13)
- Training Plan and Budget (Template 14)
- New Courses Worksheet (Template 15)

Identify Inter-Divisional/Departmental Learning Needs (5.1)

Start by reviewing Problem, Goal, and Issue Worksheets to identify learning needs that might apply to employees in multiple divisions/departments.

According to the sample data on Templates 9 and 10 in Step 2, claims managers need training on behavioral interviewing skills. Although the needs of other divisions/departments are not captured in the example, managers involved in interviewing in other divisions/departments may be able to benefit from this training as well. For example, the executive team noted a high turnover among salespeople. Certainly managers involved in hiring their replacements should be able to benefit from a class on behavioral interviewing skills.

Hence, you have a learning need that applies to employees in at least one division (Claims) and one department (Sales). In reviewing the Problem, Goal, and Issue Worksheets, you may find that this same need crops up for other managers and supervisors throughout All American Insurance as well.

Write each potential inter-divisional/departmental learning need and audience description, including positions and number of employees, on a Post-it™ Note. Place the Post-it Note on a large board or wall. Then cross off the learning need from the Problem, Goal, or Issue Worksheet.

Continue in this manner until you feel you have identified all possible learning needs that apply to employees in multiple division/departments. Then group the Post-it Notes so that related needs appear together.

For each group of related learning needs, review the positions these needs apply to so you can see whether it is possible to combine positions into a single audience for the purpose of training. In the above case, sales managers and claims managers can attend the same behavioral interviewing course.

Identify New Inter-Divisional/Departmental Courses (5.2)

Based on the training audiences you identify, group related learning needs into one or more courses on the New Course Worksheet. For an example, see the first page of Template 15 on page 65.

Then double-check your Existing Training Worksheet to make sure that learning needs are not already addressed by an existing course. For example, All American already offers a course on behavioral interviewing skills. If it isn't currently being offered, you'll need to add it to the training plan and budget.

Repeat this process for each group of related learning needs until you have a list of new courses that need to be developed.

Identify Division/Department Learning Needs (5.3)

Now you'll be examining the needs of individual divisions and departments. Review the remaining learning needs on the Problem, Goal, and Issue Worksheets for the first division/department. Write each learning need, audience description, including position, number of employees, and location, on a Post-it Note. Place the Post-it Note on a large board or wall. Then cross off the learning need from the worksheet.

Continue in this manner until you feel you have identified all possible learning needs for employees in this division/department. Next, group the Post-it Notes so that related learning needs appear together.

For each group of related learning needs, review the positions these needs apply to so you can see if it is possible to combine positions into a single audience for the purpose of training.

Based on the information you gathered in Templates 7 (page 52), 10 (page 38) and 12 (page 41) in Steps 2 and 3, you will not be able to combine positions within the Claims Division into a single audience for a course.

Identify New Division/Department Courses (5.4)

Based on the training audiences you identify, group related learning needs into one or more courses on the New Course Worksheet. For an example, see the second and third pages of Template 15 on pages 66 and 67.

You should also indicate whether the course is mandatory. Many organizations are required to provide annual safety training to meet OSHA regulations. This is one example of mandatory training. Even if you cannot link this training to solving a problem, achieving a goal, or resolving an issue, you must continue to offer it.

Now double-check your Existing Training Worksheet to make sure that learning needs aren't already addressed by an existing course. Again, if you identify a need for a course that currently isn't being offered, you'll need to add it to the training plan and budget.

Repeat this process for each group of related learning needs until you have a list of new courses that need to be developed.

Add New Courses to the Training Plan and Budget (5.5)

Add the following information for each new course to the training plan and budget:

- Proposed course

- Link to problem, goal, or issue

- Training audience

Leave the remaining columns blank for now. See the example on Template 14 on pages 68–70.

Ask yourself, "If a group of people looked at the training plan, and I wasn't there to explain it, would it be obvious how the proposed courses support solving problems, achieving goals, and resolving issues?"

Scratch off any courses that you can't link to problems, goals, and issues. Remember, you have finite resources, so you won't be able to do it all. Focus instead on mandatory training and training that supports organizational objectives.

Case Study

The next day, J.P., Ken, and Rashita are scheduled to be back in the conference room again. "Today will be another long one," J.P. sighs as she clears up the empty coffee cups, sticky napkins, and scratch paper from yesterday's meeting.

When Ken and Rashita arrive, J.P. digs right in. "We need to figure out what new courses we might need to develop this year," J.P. explains. "Let's start by identifying learning needs that might apply to more than one department or division."

"What about interviewing skills?" Rashita pipes up. "That's right," Ken adds. "Claims needs to hire more supervisors. And wasn't the VP of Sales complaining about the high turnover of salespeople in the branch offices?" J.P. writes, "How to use behavioral interviewing skills. Sales Managers, 18, Headquarters" on a Post-it Note and sticks the note to the wall. She then adds a second note for Claims.

The group then works its way through the Problem, Goal, and Issue Worksheets to identify other learning needs that might apply to employees in more than one division or department. They note each learning need on a separate Post-it Note and add it to the collection on the wall.

Next, all three work together to group related learning needs by moving Post-it Notes adjacent to each other. "It looks like we can offer a single course on behavioral interviewing skills to both the Claims Division and the Sales Department," J.P. notes as she steps back from the wall to review the group's work. "Ahhh . . . and it looks like our Hiring for Success course will fit the bill," Ken responds, tapping a pencil against his teeth and glancing down at the list of existing training courses he and Rashita compiled earlier.

The group continues this process, noting where they can use existing courses to satisfy learning needs and adding potential new courses to the training plan.

After a short break, the group turns its attention to identifying learning needs specific to a single division or department. They write each need on a Post-it Note and stick it to a blank section of the wall. J.P. then leads them in examining each need to see if any can be combined. If this is the case, the Training Department may be able to offer one course that will meet the needs of multiple target audiences. If not, the Training Department will need to offer a course specific to a single target audience.

Once again, they check the learning needs against the list of existing courses to see if they already have a course in place that will meet the need. If the need cannot be met by an existing course, Rashita adds the potential new course to the Training Plan.

J.P. breathes a sigh of relief as she shuts off the conference room light at the end of the day. "The really hard planning work is done," she thinks. "Now it's just a matter of dealing with the details. But that can wait for another day." [See Template 15 for a detailed listing of the new courses. See Template 14 for how those courses fit into the Training Plan.]

Template 15

New Courses Worksheet

Inter-Divisional/Departmental Training

Use the worksheet below to turn learning needs into possible courses.

Problem, Goal, or Issue	Learning Needs	Course	Mandatory? (Yes or No)	Training Audience
> Claims—supervisors aren't supervising. *	How to coach employees.	Coaching for Success	No	Managers, 75.
	How to mentor peers.	Peer Mentoring 101	No	Experienced employees with supervisor/manager approval, 150.
	How to organize work. How to assign work.	Work Management	No	New supervisors, 120.

Employee locations include regional offices, Claims Reporting Center, and headquarters.

*This training need may have been identified based on problems, goals, or issues experienced by other division/departments in addition to the Claims Division. This example only shows a link to the problems, goals, and issues for the Claims Division.

New Courses Worksheet

Claims Division Training

Use the worksheet below to turn learning needs into possible courses.

Problem, Goal, or Issue	Learning Needs	Course	Mandatory? (Yes or No)	Training Audience
> Adjusters are not complying with DOI regulations.	*What DOI regulations are. How DOI regulations apply to resolving auto claims.*	Auto Claims- Remaining in Compliance	No	*Auto Adjusters, 860. Regional offices.*
	What DOI regulations are. How DOI regulations apply to resolving homeowners claims.	Homeowners Claims—Remaining in Compliance	No	*Homeowners Adjusters, 400. Regional offices.*
	How often to check files. What to check. What to look for when checking files. When and how to provide feedback to adjusters.	DOI File Review	No	*Auto Claims Supervisors, 43. Homeowners Claims Supervisors, 20. Regional offices.*
> Improve customer service by reducing the time it takes to resolve a claim.	*What the steps are to resolve each type of auto claim. How to correctly complete each step. What decisions need to be made during the resolution of a claim. How to make those decisions.*	Investigating Auto Claims	No	*New Auto Adjusters, 460. Regional offices.*
		Resolving Medical Payment Claims	No	
		Resolving Collision and Comprehensive Claims	No	
		Resolving BI, GBI, and PI Claims	No	
		Resolving Auto Property Damage Claims	No	

Template 15 *(continued, p. 3)*

New Courses Worksheet

Claims Division Training

Use the worksheet below to turn learning needs into possible courses.

Problem, Goal, or Issue	Learning Needs	Course	Mandatory? (Yes or No)	Training Audience
> Improve customer service by reducing the time it takes to resolve a claim.	What are the steps to resolve each type of homeowners claim. How to correctly complete each step. What decisions need to be made during the resolution of a claim. How to make those decisions.	Investigating Homeowners Claims	No	New Homeowners Adjusters, 150. Regional offices
		Resolving Dwelling and Other Structure Claims	No	
		Resolving Personal and Scheduled Property Claims	No	
		Resolving Medical Payment Claims	No	
		Resolving Homeowners Property Damage Claims	No	
	How to use the workload-balancing application.	Introduction to Workload Balancing	No	Claims Reporting Hotline Representatives, 1,000. Claims Reporting Center.
	How to teach new claims courses.	Train the Trainer	No	Claims Trainers, 12. Claims Reporting Center.

Training Plan and Budget

New Inter-Divisional/Departmental Training

Purpose or Link to Problem, Goal, or Issue	Training Audience	Proposed Course	Delivery Method	Course Length	Exists, Develop, or Buy	Budget
> *Claims—supervisors aren't supervising.* *	Managers, 75. Regional offices. Claims Reporting Center. Headquarters.	Coaching for Success				
	Experienced employees with supervisor/manager approval, 150. Regional offices. Claims Reporting Center. Headquarters.	Peer Mentoring 101				
	New supervisors, 120. Regional offices. Claims Reporting Center. Headquarters.	Work Management				

*You may be able to link the course to other problems, goals, and issues from other division/departments. This partially completed template only shows a link to the problems, goals, and issues for the Claims Division.

Training Plan and Budget

New Claims Division Training

Purpose or Link to Problem, Goal, or Issue	Training Audience	Proposed Course	Delivery Method	Course Length	Exists, Develop, or Buy	Budget
> Adjusters are not complying with DOI regulations.	Auto Adjusters, 860. Regional offices.	Auto Claims—Remaining in Compliance				
	Homeowners Adjusters, 400. Regional offices.	Homeowners Claims—Remaining in Compliance				
	Auto Claims Supervisors, 43. Homeowners Claims Supervisors, 20. Regional offices.	DOI File Review				
> Improve customer service by reducing the time it takes to resolve a claim.	New Auto Adjusters, 460. Regional offices.	Investigating Auto Claims				
		Resolving Medical Payment Claims				
		Resolving Collision and Comprehensive Claims				
		Resolving BI, GBI, and PI Claims				
		Resolving Auto Property Damage Claims				

Training Plan and Budget

New Claims Division Training

Purpose or Link to Problem, Goal, or Issue	Training Audience	Proposed Course	Delivery Method	Course Length	Exists, Develop, or Buy	Budget
	New Homeowners Adjusters, 150, Regional offices.	Investigating Homeowners Claims				
		Resolving Dwelling and Other Structures Claims				
		Resolving Personal and Scheduled Property Claims				
		Resolving Medical Payment Claims				
		Resolving Homeowners Property Damage Claims				
	Claims Reporting Hotline Representatives, 1,000. Claims Reporting Center.	Introduction to Workload Balancing				
	Claims Trainers, 12. Claims Reporting Center. Headquarters.	Train the Trainer (10 new courses)				

Determine
Delivery Methods

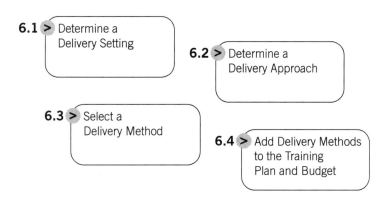

6.1 > Determine a
Delivery Setting

6.2 > Determine a
Delivery Approach

6.3 > Select a
Delivery Method

6.4 > Add Delivery Methods
to the Training
Plan and Budget

Purpose

In this step, you'll determine the optimum delivery method for each new course based on learners' needs, organizational culture and constraints, and anticipated cost. You won't be able to determine a potential budget for development and delivery until you have determined the delivery method.

Template

You will need the following template to complete this step:

- Training Plan and Budget (Template 14)

Determine a Delivery Setting (6.1)

You'll need to determine the most effective way to deliver each course from both a learning perspective and a cost perspective.

For each training audience, use the checklist below to determine whether participants will learn most effectively in a group or in an independent study setting.

Group Setting	Independent Study Setting
____ People are used to and enjoy working together on projects.	____ People are used to and prefer working independently.
____ People can't make time to learn unless they are away from their jobs.	____ People are highly motivated to make time to complete the training.
____ The organization can allow people time away from their jobs to attend training.	____ People cannot take time away from their jobs to attend training.
____ Demand for the course will be large enough to fill classes.	____ Course demand will be low; it may be difficult to fill classes.

If you checked more items in the left column, consider a group setting.

If you checked more items in the right column, consider an independent study setting.

Determine a Delivery Approach (6.2)

For each course a specific training audience needs, use the checklist below to determine whether the most effective delivery will be print or technology-based.

Print-Based Approach	Technology-Based Approach
___ There is little development time allotted for the training.	___ Development time is long, but delivery time is short and there is a large target audience.
___ The development budget is small.	
___ People tend to learn by taking notes in the margin and highlighting text.	___ The organization needs to cut travel costs of people attending training.
___ The organization cannot support technology-based training.	___ Convenience is a key driver of whether people can attend training.
___ People are not comfortable with technology.	___ The organization can support technology-based training.
	___ People are comfortable with technology.

Training Budgets Step-by-Step. Copyright © 2004 by John Wiley & Sons, Inc. Reproduced by permission of Pfeiffer, an Imprint of Wiley. www.pfeiffer.com

If you checked more items in the left column, consider a print-based approach.

If you checked more items in the right column, consider a technology-based approach.

Select a Delivery Method (6.3)

Once you've determined the most appropriate setting (group or independent study) and the most effective delivery approach (print or technology-based) for a particular course, review the chart at the bottom of the next page.

The following definitions will help you to understand the various delivery options.

- *Asynchronous Internet-Based Classroom Training:* Learners log on to the Internet-based course when it is convenient for them (they need not be logged on simultaneously) to learn new information and participate in bulletin board discussions and activities with the trainer and their classmates who may all be in different locations.

- *Audiographics Training:* Audiographics training is similar to learning over a conference call with one addition: learners and the trainer also can create computer-generated graphics to share with other sites.

- *Audio Teletraining:* Audio teletraining is similar to learning over a conference call. Learners can hear the trainer and each other, and the trainer can hear learners.

- *Computer-Based Training (CBT)/Web-Based Training Self-Paced CBT/WBT :* Learners work at their own pace to learn new information, participate in practice activities, and take tests provided electronically on a CD-ROM, over the Internet, or over their company's intranet.

- *Classroom Training:* Learners meet face-to-face with the trainer and their classmates to learn new information and participate in discussions and activities.

- *Coaching/Structured On-the-Job Training (OJT):* Learners work under the direction of a designated expert who serves as a coach to learn new information and skills.

- *Electronic Performance Support System (EPSS):* Learners access electronic information as needed in the course of performing their jobs to look up steps and procedures. A good example is online help for Microsoft Word®.

- *Interactive TV:* Learners can see and hear the trainer by watching a video monitor. The trainer can receive immediate feedback from learners via an audio system, a keypad viewer response system, telephone, or fax. The trainer cannot, however, see the learners.

- *Job Aid:* Learners look up how to do a specific task on a cheat sheet.

- *Paper-Based Self-Paced Training:* Learners work at their own pace to learn new information, participate in practice activities, and take tests provided in a printed workbook.

- *Synchronous Internet-Based Classroom Training:* Learners log on to the Internet-based course simultaneously at a designated time to learn new information and participate in discussions and activities with the trainer and their classmates, who may be in different locations.

- *Video Teleconferencing:* Learners can see and hear the trainer by watching a video monitor. The trainer can also see and hear learners.

Training Delivery Options

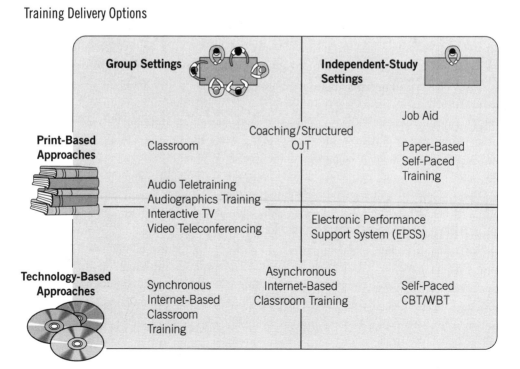

As you make your selection, consider that what works best for learners may not be the most cost-effective approach. Before you settle on a delivery method, assess the tradeoffs between the optimum setting for learners and the most cost-effective delivery method for the course.

For example, learners in your organization may learn best in a group setting because of the collegial nature of your corporate culture. If, on the other hand, they are located all over the world, selecting an asynchronous technology-based delivery method for a course, while not optimum for learners, may be more cost-effective.

You'll also need to consider organizational constraints. For example, learners may only be able to get away from their jobs for a half-day at a time. This may make classroom training impractical if learners have to travel, even locally, to attend training.

Also note that in some cases a blended learning approach combining such delivery methods as WBT and classroom training might be appropriate.

For each course included in your plan, follow these same steps:

1. Determine the delivery setting (group or independent study) based on target audience characteristics.

2. Determine the delivery approach (print- or technology-based) for each course you plan to offer this target audience based on organizational constraints.

3. Weigh the pros and cons to select a delivery method for the course.

Add Delivery Methods to the Training Plan and Budget (6.4)

For each course, note the delivery method you've selected in the Training Plan and Budget. The remaining columns are still blank. See the example of Template 14 on pages 78–80.

Case Study

Fast forward to a week after the last meeting. Ken and Rashita are sitting in J.P.'s office feeling refreshed and ready to tackle the next step.

J.P. assigns each several new courses to focus on. They'll need to do an analysis to figure out what might be the best delivery method for their assigned courses. The tricky part will be balancing learners' needs with the cost of the delivery method and the constraints of the organization.

For example, the call center culture is very social. Employees regularly participate in potluck lunches, contests, and pep talks. In fact, on J.P.'s last visit, the smell of Pho was wafting from the break room. Apparently, one of the call center adjusters had prepared her favorite food to share with her co-workers.

This strong social culture would typically indicate that the most effective learning would take place in a group setting, most likely the classroom. However, J.P. plans to deliver the course on remaining in compliance with DOI regulations to auto adjusters via WBT.

She made this decision for several reasons. First, once the initial training of auto adjusters is complete, she may not have enough learners to fill a class on a regular basis. Also, this topic is critical enough that she can't wait until she has a critical mass of people who need the training to offer it. She also took into account that this group is comfortable with technology and that the IT Department is prepared to support a WBT implementation.

Once J.P., Ken, and Rashita have decided on a delivery method for each new course, J.P. adds this information to the training plan. [See Template 14 for a sample of filled-in delivery methods for new training.]

Training Plan and Budget

New Inter-Divisional/Departmental Training

Purpose or Link to Problem, Goal, or Issue	Training Audience	Proposed Course	Delivery Method	Course Length	Exists, Develop, or Buy	Budget
> Claims—supervisors aren't supervising.*	Managers, 75. Regional offices. Claims Reporting Center. Headquarters.	Coaching for Success	Audio Teletraining			
	Experienced employees with supervisor/manager approval, 150. Regional offices. Claims Reporting Center. Headquarters.	Peer Mentoring 101	WBT			
	New supervisors, 120. Regional offices. Claims Reporting Center. Headquarters.	Work Management	Self-Paced			

*You may be able to link the course to other problems, goals, and issues from other division/departments. This partially completed template only shows a link to the problems, goals, and issues for the Claims Division.

Training Plan and Budget

New Claims Division Training

Purpose or Link to Problem, Goal, or Issue	Training Audience	Proposed Course	Delivery Method	Course Length	Exists, Develop, or Buy	Budget
> Adjusters are not complying with DOI regulations.	Auto Adjusters, 860. Regional offices.	Auto Claims—Remaining in Compliance	WBT			
	Homeowners Adjusters, 400. Regional offices.	Homeowners Claims—Remaining in Compliance	WBT			
	Auto Claims Supervisors, 43. Homeowners Claims Supervisors, 20. Regional offices.	DOI File Review	WBT			
> Improve customer service by reducing the time it takes to resolve a claim.	New Auto Adjusters, 460. Regional offices.	Investigating Auto Claims	Classroom			
		Resolving Medical Payment Claims	Classroom			
		Resolving Collision and Comprehensive Claims	Classroom			
		Resolving BI, GBI, and PI Claims	Classroom			
		Resolving Auto Property Damage Claims	Classroom			

Template 14 *(continued, p. 6)*

Training Plan and Budget

New Claims Division Training

Purpose or Link to Problem, Goal, or Issue	Training Audience	Proposed Course	Delivery Method	Course Length	Exists, Develop, or Buy	Budget
	New Homeowners Adjusters, 150. Regional offices.	Investigating Homeowners Claims	Classroom			
		Resolving Dwelling and Other Structures Claims	Classroom			
		Resolving Personal and Scheduled Property Claims	Classroom			
		Resolving Medical Payment Claims	Classroom			
		Resolving Homeowners Property Damage Claims	Classroom			
	Claims Reporting Hotline Representatives, 1,000. Claims Reporting Center.	Introduction to Workload Balancing	CBT			
	Claims Trainers, 12. Claims Reporting Center. Headquarters.	Train the Trainer (10 new courses)	Classroom			

Determine Course Length

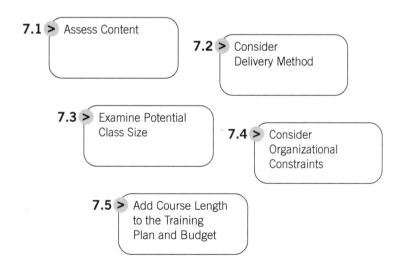

7.1 > Assess Content

7.2 > Consider Delivery Method

7.3 > Examine Potential Class Size

7.4 > Consider Organizational Constraints

7.5 > Add Course Length to the Training Plan and Budget

Purpose

You won't be able to determine a potential budget if you don't know how long each course will be. For example, you'll certainly need to plan a larger budget for a three-day course than you will for a three-hour course. So in this step you'll need to make some educated guesses on anticipated course length.

Template

You will need the following template to complete this step:

- Training Plan and Budget (Template 14)

Assess Content (7.1)

To get a feel for how long it will take to teach the content, talk to subject-matter experts. They generally have a pretty good idea of how complex and difficult it is to learn something and thus how long it might take someone to learn it.

For example, teaching learners to use a new email system might take two hours. In contrast, teaching them to use a proprietary claims processing application might take two days.

Consider Delivery Method (7.2)

Synchronous delivery methods, where there is real-time interaction between learners, and between learners and the instructor, take longer than self-paced delivery methods. This is because you need to allow time for discussions and question-and-answer periods. In addition, there is always a social component that is part of these sessions.

When you talk to subject-matter experts, assume that the time they recommend to learn a particular skill is based on real-time training. You can generally shave one-third to one-half off this time if the training will be self-paced.

Examine Potential Class Size (7.3)

If you plan to train a large number of employees (more than twenty) simultaneously, add about one-fourth to one-third to the time cited by subject-matter experts. This is because discussions and question-and-answer periods will take longer with more people participating. In addition, it will take longer to organize learning activities and to get the class back on track after breaks.

Consider Organizational Constraints (7.4)

Organizational constraints also play a part in course length. For example, some organizations are unwilling or unable to release employees to attend training for more than a half-day at a time. In a retail setting, training may need to be completed during the one-hour store meeting that occurs before the store opens. You'll need to find out what, if any, constraints impact course length.

If you can't cover all the material implied by the objective in the time allowed, you may need to break up one course into multiple shorter modules.

Add Course Length to the Training Plan and Budget (7.5)

Note the length of each course on the Training Plan and Budget. The remaining columns are still blank. See the example of Template 14 on pages 85–87.

Case Study

With a delivery method identified for each course, J.P. assigns Ken and Rashita to determine the projected length of each course. "This will be a total wild guess!" Ken complains. "How can we figure out the length of a course we haven't even started designing?"

"I know. I know," J.P. agrees. "But we can't come up with a budget unless we have an educated guess as to how long each course will be. Just do the best you can."

A pop-up meeting reminder flashes on J.P.'s computer screen. Time to meet with the subject-matter expert who will provide the content for the DOI regulations WBT course J.P. is planning for auto adjusters. J.P. grabs a notebook and pen and walks to the elevators with Ken and Rashita as she heads to the meeting.

Myron Glick turns to greet J.P. at her knock on the frame of his cubicle. "Let's meet outside. This way I can get out of this cramped cubicle, and we can enjoy the sunshine," Myron suggests. J.P. follows Myron out to a rough-hewn picnic table in All American's courtyard.

With the sun warm on their backs, J.P. and Myron discuss the DOI compliance course. They figure the course will need to include what the regulations are and why they are important. They also figure they'll need some scenarios so learners can see how regulations come into play during the claims-resolution process. And, of course, there will need to be an end-of-course test to make sure learners have mastered the material.

Once they've sketched out the course at a very high level, J.P. and Myron estimate the course length. "Sounds like about an hour will do it," J.P. surmises. "WBT is typically faster than instructor-led training. What do you think, Myron?"

Myron agrees an hour sounds about right.

Back in her office, J.P. notes "1 hour" in the training plan beside the Auto Claims—Remaining in Compliance course. She'll fill in the rest of the information in the Course Length column once Ken and Rashita have completed their research. [See the sample of Template 14 with the course length filled in for new courses.]

Training Plan and Budget

New Inter-Divisional/Departmental Training

Purpose or Link to Problem, Goal, or Issue	Training Audience	Proposed Course	Delivery Method	Course Length	Exists, Develop, or Buy	Budget
> *Claims—supervisors aren't supervising.* *	*Managers, 75. Regional offices. Claims Reporting Center. Headquarters.*	*Coaching for Success*	*Audio Teletraining*	2 sessions of 4 hours each		
	Experienced employees with supervisor/manager approval, 150. Regional offices. Claims Reporting Center. Headquarters.	*Peer Mentoring 101*	*WBT*	3 hours		
	New supervisors, 120. Regional offices. Claims Reporting Center. Headquarters.	*Work Management*	*Self-Paced*	2 hours plus assignments performed over 2 weeks		

*You may be able to link the course to other problems, goals, and issues from other division/departments. This partially completed template only shows a link to the problems, goals, and issues for the Claims Division.

Template 14 *(continued, p. 5)*

Training Plan and Budget

New Claims Division Training

Purpose or Link to Problem, Goal, or Issue	Training Audience	Proposed Course	Delivery Method	Course Length	Exists, Develop, or Buy	Budget
> Adjusters are not complying with DOI regulations.	Auto Adjusters, 860. Regional offices.	Auto Claims—Remaining in Compliance	WBT	1 hour		
	Homeowners Adjusters, 400. Regional offices.	Homeowners Claims—Remaining in Compliance	WBT	1 hour		
	Auto Claims Supervisors, 43. Homeowners Claims Supervisors, 20. Regional offices.	DOI File Review	WBT	2 hours		
> Improve customer service by reducing the time it takes to resolve a claim.	New Auto Adjusters, 460. Regional offices.	Investigating Auto Claims	Classroom	1 day		
		Resolving Medical Payment Claims	Classroom	2 days		
		Resolving Collision and Comprehensive Claims	Classroom	2 days		
		Resolving BI, GBI, and PI Claims	Classroom	3 days		
		Resolving Auto Property Damage Claims	Classroom	2 days		

Training Plan and Budget

New Claims Division Training

Purpose or Link to Problem, Goal, or Issue	Training Audience	Proposed Course	Delivery Method	Course Length	Exists, Develop, or Buy	Budget
	New Homeowners Adjusters, 150. Regional offices.	Investigating Homeowners Claims	Classroom	1 day		
		Resolving Dwelling and Other Structures Claims	Classroom	2 days		
		Resolving Personal and Scheduled Property Claims	Classroom	2 days		
		Resolving Medical Payment Claims	Classroom	2 days		
		Resolving Homeowners Property Damage Claims	Classroom	2 days		
	Claims Reporting Hotline Representatives, 1,000. Claims Reporting Center.	Introduction to Workload Balancing	CBT	1.5 hours		
	Claims Trainers, 12. Claims Reporting Center. Headquarters.	Train the Trainer (10 new courses)	Classroom	19 days		

Decide Whether to Make or Buy the Training

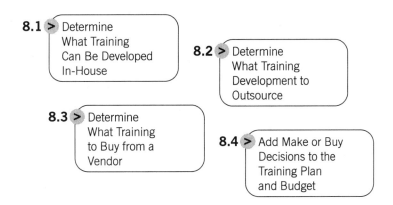

8.1 > Determine What Training Can Be Developed In-House

8.2 > Determine What Training Development to Outsource

8.3 > Determine What Training to Buy from a Vendor

8.4 > Add Make or Buy Decisions to the Training Plan and Budget

Purpose

Once you've determined the delivery method and length of each new course, it is time to assess in-house resources and potentially available funding to determine whether you should make or buy each course.

Template

You will need the following template to complete this step:

- Training Plan and Budget (Template 14)

Determine What Training Can Be Developed In-House (8.1)

Consider developing training in-house if you have available the following resources:

Resources	Caveats
Instructional design expertise	Avoid assigning development responsibilities to subject-matter experts. They may know the topic, but that doesn't mean they know how to teach the topic so others can learn. Make sure to pair subject-matter experts with an instructional design resource.
Time	If you are trying to roll out a large curriculum in a short time, you may need to supplement your staff with outside resources.
Content expertise	If you do not have the content expertise in-house, you may need to purchase a generic course from a vendor or have a vendor develop a custom course that meets the needs of your organization.

Determine What Training Development to Outsource (8.2)

Use the checklist below to determine whether it makes sense to retain an instructional design firm to help you develop training.

Outsource training development if. . .

☐ You need to teach employees something that is proprietary to your organization (for example, a customized software application, product knowledge, job-specific business processes and procedures) or it is more expensive to purchase a generic course from a vendor, *and*

☐ You don't have the instructional design expertise to develop training in-house, *or*

☐ You don't have the time to develop training in-house, *or*

☐ You don't have the content expertise to develop training in-house, *and*

☐ You have the budget, *or*

☐ The per-person cost is not extravagant (you have a lot of people who need the same training at the same time or over time; the training will be repeated periodically for the foreseeable future).

If you won't be teaching employees something that is proprietary to your organization, it probably makes more sense to buy and customize, if necessary, an off-the-shelf course. This is because you can begin to offer the training sooner. Plus, it is often less expensive to buy a generic course than to outsource custom development. Finally, often off-the-shelf courses have the benefit of being able to produce proven results. In many cases, vendors have tested them with clients to show that the training works. You'll need to pilot and evaluate the results of a custom course to ensure that it works.

If the course will be covering proprietary content, it makes sense to outsource development if you don't have the instructional design or content expertise, or the time to develop it in-house, and you do have the budget. If budget is not available, you'll need to figure out a way to develop it in-house or put off development until funds become available.

You should also make sure that you have enough people who need the training to make it worth the cost of outsourcing custom development. It is very hard to justify the cost of custom development for a small group of people unless the cost of making a mistake is very high.

For example, poor training was cited as the cause of a passenger train accident that killed one person and injured 198 others, according to the Transportation Safety Board of Canada. An onboard system detected the problem and sounded an alarm twenty-nine hours before the derailment. Due to inadequate training, operations and maintenance employees concluded that the failure was in the warning system and disconnected it. In this case, even if there were only a few operations and maintenance employees, it would have been well worth the cost of hiring an experienced instructional design firm to design the training, rather than trying to pull something together in-house if instructional design expertise was not available.

Determine What Training to Buy from a Vendor (8.3)

Use the checklist below to help determine whether it makes sense to purchase a generic course from a vendor.

Buy a generic course if. . .

☐ You can find a course that meets your needs with little or no customization, *and*

☐ You have the budget, *and*

☐ You want a course that has been tested and shown to produce results, *or*

☐ You don't have the instructional design expertise to develop training in-house, *or*

☐ You don't have the time to develop training in-house, *or*

☐ You don't have the content expertise to develop training in-house, *and*

☐ The per person cost is not extravagant (you have a lot of people who need the same training at the same time or over time; the training will be repeated periodically for the foreseeable future).

Of course, if you can't find a course that meets your needs, you won't have the option of buying the course.

Again, you need to have budget available. Buying a course becomes a moot point if budget money is not available.

You should also make sure the course is cost-effective. Does it really make sense to buy a course that will only be applicable to a small number of people? In this case, you may be able to find a public seminar or a community college course you can send this group to that will be more cost-effective then licensing the rights to an off-the-shelf course.

Finally, if you don't have the instructional design or content expertise or the time to develop a generic course in-house, buying may be your best option. The cost of custom development of a generic course may be higher than the cost to buy the course. Also, the vendors of many off-the-shelf courses can provide guarantees from past clients that their training works. You'll need to pilot and evaluate a custom course to ensure that it works.

Add Make or Buy Decisions to the Training Plan and Budget (8.4)

On the Training Plan and Budget, indicate whether you plan to make or buy each new course. Leave the last column blank for now. See the example of Template 14 on pages 94–96.

Case Study

J.P. carefully places a steaming mug of coffee on a coaster as she peruses the training plan. Now she'll need to decide whether the Training Department should use its resources to design and develop the courses, buy generic courses from a vendor, or hire a vendor to design and develop the courses on All American's behalf.

"Hmmm. . . . what should we do about the WBT on DOI regulations for auto adjusters?" J.P. muses. "We have the subject-matter expertise to develop the content in-house in the form of Myron Glick. We can draw on in-house instructional design, graphics, and programming expertise. And the course shouldn't take too long to develop. We might as well develop this course in-house," J.P. concludes.

In the same way, it makes sense to develop the DOI regulations for homeowners insurance adjusters in-house as well. Many of the regulations are the same. Plus, J.P. suspects the programming team will be able to reuse some of the code from the auto adjuster version of this course.

On the other hand, Coaching for Success is probably a course J.P. can buy from a vendor and customize, if needed. J.P. jots a note to remember to ask Rashita to look into finding just such a course.

Course by course, J.P. works through the training plan, deciding whether it makes more sense to make or buy each. [See the partial example on Template 14 for the results of J.P.'s work in this step.]

Training Plan and Budget

New Inter-Divisional/Departmental Training

Purpose or Link to Problem, Goal, or Issue	Training Audience	Proposed Course	Delivery Method	Course Length	Exists, Develop, or Buy	Budget
> Claims—supervisors aren't supervising. *	Managers, 75. Regional offices. Claims Reporting Center. Headquarters.	Coaching for Success	Audio Teletraining	2 sessions of 4 hours each	Buy course from vendor.	
	Experienced employees with supervisor/manager approval, 150. Regional offices. Claims Reporting Center. Headquarters.	Peer Mentoring 101	WBT	3 hours	Develop in-house.	
	New supervisors, 120. Regional offices. Claims Reporting Center. Headquarters.	Work Management	Self-Paced	2 hours plus assignments performed over 2 weeks	Develop in-house.	

*You may be able to link the course to other problems, goals, and issues from other division/departments. This partially completed template only shows a link to the problems, goals, and issues for the Claims Division.

Training Plan and Budget

New Claims Division Training

Purpose or Link to Problem, Goal, or Issue	Training Audience	Proposed Course	Delivery Method	Course Length	Exists, Develop, or Buy	Budget
> Adjusters are not complying with DOI regulations.	Auto Adjusters, 860. Regional offices.	Auto Claims—Remaining in Compliance	WBT	1 hour	Develop in-house.	
	Homeowners Adjusters, 400. Regional offices.	Homeowners Claims—Remaining in Compliance	WBT	1 hour	Develop in-house.	
	Auto Claims Supervisors, 43. Homeowners Claims 88 Supervisors, 20. Regional offices.	DOI File Review	WBT	2 hours	Develop in-house.	
> Improve customer service by reducing the time it takes to resolve a claim.	New Auto Adjusters, 460. Regional offices.	Investigating Auto Claims	Classroom	1 day	Outsource development.	
		Resolving Medical Payment Claims	Classroom	2 days	Outsource development.	
		Resolving Collision and Comprehensive Claims	Classroom	2 days	Outsource development.	
		Resolving BI, GBI, and PI Claims	Classroom	3 days	Outsource development.	
		Resolving Auto Property Damage Claims	Classroom	2 days	Outsource development.	

Training Plan and Budget

New Claims Division Training

Purpose or Link to Problem, Goal, or Issue	Training Audience	Proposed Course	Delivery Method	Course Length	Exists, Develop, or Buy	Budget
	New Homeowners Adjusters, 150. Regional offices.	Investigating Homeowners Claims	Classroom	1 day	Outsource development.	
		Resolving Dwelling and Other Structures Claims	Classroom	2 days	Outsource development.	
		Resolving Personal and Scheduled Property Claims	Classroom	2 days	Outsource development.	
		Resolving Medical Payment Claims	Classroom	2 days	Outsource development.	
		Resolving Homeowners Property Damage Claims	Classroom	2 days	Outsource development.	
	Claims Reporting Hotline Representatives, 1,000. Claims Reporting Center.	Introduction to Workload Balancing	CBT	1.5 hours	Develop in-house.	
	Claims Trainers, 12. Claims Reporting Center. Headquarters.	Train the Trainer (10 new courses)	Classroom	19 days	Develop in-house.	

Create a
Training Budget

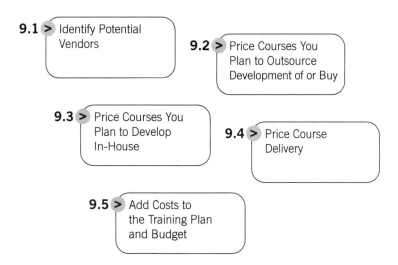

9.1 > Identify Potential
Vendors

9.2 > Price Courses You
Plan to Outsource
Development of or Buy

9.3 > Price Courses You
Plan to Develop
In-House

9.4 > Price Course
Delivery

9.5 > Add Costs to
the Training Plan
and Budget

Purpose

Now it is time to cost out the training plan. You'll need to work with potential vendors from whom you plan to purchase a course or outsource instructional design services from to figure out the cost of courses you'll buy. You'll also need to figure out the cost of courses you'll develop in-house and the cost of delivery.

Template

You will need the following template to complete this step:

- Training Plan and Budget (Template 14)

Identify Potential Vendors (9.1)

For each course you plan to purchase, you can identify potential vendors in the following ways:

- Ask colleagues for recommendations
- Check out the American Society for Training and Development's online buyer's guide at www.astd.org
- Check out the International Society for Performance Improvement's online buyer's guide at www.ispi.org
- Check out *Training* magazine's online buyer's guide at www.trainingmag.com
- Sort through any marketing materials you may have received.

Price Courses You Plan to Outsource Development of or Buy (9.2)

Contact vendors and describe the course. At a minimum, you'll need to be prepared to answer the following questions:

- Who is your target audience (position, size, location, and so forth)?
- What is the course?
- What is the purpose of the course?
- What is the length of the course?
- How do you plan to deliver the course (classroom, WBT, or however)?

In order to provide you with a more accurate estimate, vendors may ask additional questions, depending on the situation.

For example, if you plan to hire a vendor to develop a three-hour Web-based course on a proprietary system, the vendor may also need access to any system documentation your organization has. This will help the vendor assess how much additional information will have to be collected to develop the course. In this case, the more information the vendor needs to collect in addition to what's been documented, the higher the cost of the course.

Once you've answered the vendor's questions, ask for a rough estimate of cost.

Price Courses You Plan to Develop In-House (9.3)

Besides salary costs for in-house training and instructional design staff, you might have additional costs associated with developing courses in-house. These costs could include any of the following:

- Travel for instructional designers to gather information
- The purchase of books or reprints of articles needed to research the course topic
- Course materials, such as binders or videotapes, that must be purchased for a course
- Reproduction of course materials
- Authoring software to build the course

Price Course Delivery (9.4)

As you price the cost of delivering each course, think about the delivery method chosen, how many sessions you'll offer, and what the potential cost is per session. Costs associated with delivery could include the following:

- Travel for learners to attend the training

- Travel for instructors to deliver the training

- Outside facilitators hired to deliver the training

- Meals or snacks provided with the training

- Facilities, such as hotel rooms, needed to deliver the training

- Equipment or software, such as conferencing software, flip charts and markers, to support course delivery

- Technical support required to support course delivery

- Delivery of course materials to the training site

- Administrative costs, such as registration, arranging for facilities, tracking attendance, and so on

- Storage/warehouse space to house training materials

- Upgrade of servers to support Web-delivered training

It is also a good idea to look up historical data on what training expenses have been paid in the past. This will help ensure you don't leave anything out. It will also give you a benchmark to gauge your budget against.

Add Costs to the Training Plan and Budget (9.5)

Tally up the costs for each course. Then note the cost of each course in the last column of the Training Plan and Budget. Sum the costs of all courses and you should have a pretty accurate idea of the total amount required to implement your training plan. See the example of Template 14 on pages 102–104.

Since things never go according to plan, you might want to add a fudge factor of one-third to your bottom line. This should help ensure that you can meet your training goals without exceeding your training budget.

Case Study

Now comes the part J.P. dreads—figuring out the budget. "Budgeting always feels so over-whelming and imprecise," J.P. sighs.

She starts by looking at the actual dollars the Training Department spent last year. She then makes an educated guess as to how this coming year's plan compares to last year. "Hmm. . . .it feels like this year we'll be offering about 20 percent more in terms of days of training than last year. Theoretically, the budget should be about 20 percent more." J.P. taps the numbers into her trusty calculator and notes the result on a pad.

Next, J.P. will need to figure out the cost of each course and add them up to come up with a total budget for the year. She'll compare this total budget to the number she wrote on her pad to see how closely they match. Then she'll spend some time adjusting both until she feels com-fortable that they reconcile and the budget is something All American can live with. "There is as much intuition involved as there is math," J.P. notes.

J.P. can easily pull budget numbers for existing courses that have been offered in the past. If she has selected vendors for courses she plans to buy, they should have been able to provide her with estimates. And she has a pretty good idea what it will cost for her staff to design and develop courses she's committed the department to make, as well as the cost of course delivery.

J.P. works on the budget in spurts, playing with the numbers. Since life never goes accord-ing to plan, J.P. finalizes the budget by adding a fudge factor of one-third to the bottom line. This makes her feel more comfortable that the Training Department will be able to deliver on its commitments to All American within budget. [See the Budget column in Template 14 for the results of J.P.'s work in this step.]

Training Plan and Budget

New Inter-Divisional/Departmental Training

Purpose or Link to Problem, Goal, or Issue	Training Audience	Proposed Course	Delivery Method	Course Length	Exists, Develop, or Buy	Budget
> Claims—supervisors aren't supervising.*	Managers, 75. Regional offices. Claims Reporting Center. Headquarters.	Coaching for Success	Audio Teletraining	2 sessions of 4 hours each	Buy course from vendor.	$25,000
	Experienced employees with supervisor/manager approval, 150. Regional offices. Claims Reporting Center. Headquarters.	Peer Mentoring 101	WBT	3 hours	Develop in-house.	$75,000
	New supervisors, 120. Regional offices. Claims Reporting Center. Headquarters.	Work Management	Self-Paced	2 hours plus assignments performed over 2 weeks	Develop in-house.	$8,000
Total Budget for New Inter-Divisional/Departmental Training						$108,000

*You may be able to link the course to other problems, goals, and issues from other division/departments. This partially completed template only shows a link to the problems, goals, and issues for the Claims Division.

Training Plan and Budget

New Claims Division Training

Purpose or Link to Problem, Goal, or Issue	Training Audience	Proposed Course	Delivery Method	Course Length	Exists, Develop, or Buy	Budget
> Adjusters are not complying with DOI regulations.	Auto Adjusters, 860. Regional offices.	Auto Claims—Remaining in Compliance	WBT	1 hour	Develop in-house.	$12,000
	Homeowners Adjusters, 400. Regional offices.	Homeowners Claims—Remaining in Compliance	WBT	1 hour	Develop in-house.	$12,000
	Auto Claims Supervisors, 43. Homeowners Claims Supervisors, 20. Regional offices.	DOI File Review	WBT	2 hours	Develop in-house.	$17,000
> Improve customer service by reducing the time it takes to resolve a claim.	New Auto Adjusters, 460. Regional offices.	Investigating Auto Claims	Classroom	1 day	Outsource development.	$35,000
		Resolving Medical Payment Claims	Classroom	2 days	Outsource development.	$50,000
		Resolving Collision and Comprehensive Claims	Classroom	2 days	Outsource development.	$50,000
		Resolving BI, GBI, and PI Claims	Classroom	3 days	Outsource development.	$65,000
		Resolving Auto Property Damage Claims	Classroom	2 days	Outsource development.	$50,000

Training Plan and Budget

New Claims Division Training

Purpose or Link to Problem, Goal, or Issue	Training Audience	Proposed Course	Delivery Method	Course Length	Exists, Develop, or Buy	Budget
	New Homeowners Adjusters, 150. Regional offices.	Investigating Homeowners Claims	Classroom	1 day	Outsource development.	$35,000
		Resolving Dwelling and Other Structures Claims	Classroom	2 days	Outsource development.	$50,000
		Resolving Personal and Scheduled Property Claims	Classroom	2 days	Outsource development.	$50,000
		Resolving Medical Payment Claims	Classroom	2 days	Outsource development.	$50,000
		Resolving Homeowners Property Damage Claims	Classroom	2 days	Outsource development.	$50,000
	Claims Reporting Hotline Representatives, 1,000. Claims Reporting Center.	Introduction to Workload Balancing	CBT	1.5 hours	Develop in-house.	$18,000
	Claims Trainers, 12. Claims Reporting Center. Headquarters.	Train the Trainer (10 new courses)	Classroom	19 days	Develop in-house.	$27,000
					Total Budget for New Claims Training	$571,000

Prepare to Present the Training Plan and Budget

10.1 > Prepare to Present the Training Plan and Budget

Purpose

With a first draft of the training plan and budget ready to go, you'll need to make sure that you are absolutely prepared to present it and to answer anticipated questions.

Templates

You will need the following templates to complete this step:

- Division/Department Manager—Problem Worksheet (Template 7)
- Division/Department Manager—Goal Worksheet (Template 10)

- Division/Department Manager—Issue Worksheet (Template 12)
- Existing Training Worksheet (Template 13)
- Training Plan and Budget (Template 14)
- New Courses Worksheet (Template 15)

Prepare to Present the Training Plan and Budget (10.1)

Undoubtedly you'll be called on to present your plan to the executive team, or at least to your boss. Review the questions below to ensure that you are prepared. You may need to refer to interview data, such as operational results that will indicate a problem has been solved, to prepare an answer to each before the presentation.

1. How do the proposed courses support solving problems, achieving goals, and resolving issues?

2. Is training the appropriate strategy to solve the problem?

3. Why is the delivery method chosen the most appropriate? Is it the most cost-effective? If not, what makes it a better choice than the more cost-effective approach?

4. What is the cost of developing the training in-house versus buying the training or the design and development services?

5. What is the cost per learner of training versus the cost of not training?

6. What is the bottom-line benefit to the organization of training?

Note that if you expect pushback on a particular course, you might want to determine the cost of not providing the training. To do this, you'll need to work with division/department managers and, in some cases, executives to figure out the cost of not solving the problem, achieving the goal, or resolving the issue.

For example, if providing customer service training is linked to customer loyalty, how many customers do you anticipate losing if the organization fails to provide the training? What does it cost your organization to gain a new customer? Undoubtedly, someone in marketing or sales has these figures at his or her fingertips.

You should also consider non-financial costs, such as employee morale.

Case Study

J.P., Ken, and Rashita reconvene in the conference room one last time before J.P. presents the training plan to her boss for initial approval. J.P. wants to be certain that she can answer all of her boss's anticipated questions.

They review the plan course-by-course, making sure that J.P. can clearly explain how the course will support solving the problems, achieving the goals, and addressing the issues J.P. identified in her needs assessment.

J.P. also must be prepared to address such concerns as whether training is the right answer and what the cost of *not* training might be.

As the meeting concludes, J.P. thanks Ken and Rashita for their help. The initial plan is done. While it might change before it is finally approved and again over the course of the year as All American's needs and priorities change, J.P. feels confident it will provide a good foundation on which to base future decisions. [The sample of Template 14 on the following pages shows a complete plan and budget for both existing and new training.]

Template 14

Training Plan and Budget

Existing Inter-Divisional/Departmental Training

Purpose or Link to Problem, Goal, or Issue	Training Audience	Proposed Course	Delivery Method	Course Length	Exists, Develop, or Buy	Budget
> Identify and address harassing behavior.	New employees, 400. Regional offices. Claims Reporting Center. Headquarters.	Avoiding Harassment	WBT	3 hours	Ongoing.	Not applicable.
> Orient new employees to company culture and policies.	New employees, 400. Regional offices. Claims Reporting Center. Headquarters.	New Employee Orientation	WBT	2 hours	Ongoing.	$40,000
			Classroom	1 day		
> Claims Division—need to hire additional supervisors to provide adjusters with the support they need to improve customer service by reducing the time it takes to resolve a claim.	Managers and supervisors involved in hiring, 80. Regional offices. Claims Reporting Center. Headquarters.	Hiring for Success	Classroom	1 day	Ongoing.	$40,000

*This example only shows links to problems, goals, and issues the Claims Division will be involved in addressing. Your plan would also show links to problems, goals, and issues other division/departments will be involved in addressing.

Template 14 (continued, p. 2)

Training Plan and Budget

Existing Inter-Divisional/Departmental Training

Purpose or Link to Problem, Goal, or Issue	Training Audience	Proposed Course	Delivery Method	Course Length	Exists, Develop, or Buy	Budget
> Claims Division—need to provide new supervisors with basic skills. Supervisors lack skills to evaluate work and provide employees with performance feedback.	New Supervisors, 75. Regional offices. Claims Reporting Center. Headquarters.	Managing Performance	Classroom	1 day	Ongoing.	$40,000
	New managers and supervisors, 30. Regional offices. Claims Reporting Center. Headquarters.	Conducting Performance Appraisals	Classroom	1 day	Ongoing.	$5,000
				Total Budget for Existing Inter-Divisional/Departmental Training		$125,000

*This example only shows links to problems, goals, and issues the Claims Division will be involved in addressing. Your plan would also show links to problems, goals, and issues other division/departments will be involved in addressing.

Training Plan and Budget

Existing Claims Division Training

Purpose or Link to Problem, Goal, or Issue	Training Audience	Proposed Course	Delivery Method	Course Length	Exists, Develop, or Buy	Budget
> Claims Division—adjusters are not complying with DOI regulations.	New Claims Adjusters, 100. Regional offices.	Introduction to DOI Regulations.	WBT	2 hours	Ongoing.	Not applicable.
> Ensure investigators are current on the latest insurance fraud schemes.	Special Investigators, 10. Headquarters.	Insurance Fraud Investigation	Classroom	4 hours	Ongoing.	$10,000
> Maintain customer service ratings.	New Claims Adjusters and Claims Reporting Hotline Representatives, 250. Regional offices. Claims Reporting Center.	Achieving Outstanding Customer Service	Classroom	2 hours	Ongoing.	$500,000
					Total Budget for Existing Claims Training	$510,000

Training Plan and Budget

New Inter-Divisional/Departmental Training

Purpose or Link to Problem, Goal, or Issue	Training Audience	Proposed Course	Delivery Method	Course Length	Exists, Develop, or Buy	Budget
> Claims—supervisors aren't supervising. *	Managers, 75. Regional offices. Claims Reporting Center. Headquarters.	Coaching for Success	Audio Teletraining	2 sessions of 4 hours each	Buy course from vendor.	$25,000
	Experienced employees with supervisor/manager approval, 150. Regional offices. Claims Reporting Center. Headquarters.	Peer Mentoring 101	WBT	3 hours	Develop in-house.	$75,000
	New supervisors, 120. Regional offices. Claims Reporting Center. Headquarters.	Work Management	Self-Paced	2 hours plus assignments performed over 2 weeks	Develop in-house.	$8,000
					Total Budget for New Inter-Divisional/Departmental Training	$108,000

*You may be able to link the course to other problems, goals, and issues from other division/departments. This partially completed template only shows a link to the problems, goals, and issues for the Claims Division.

Training Plan and Budget

New Claims Division Training

Purpose or Link to Problem, Goal, or Issue	Training Audience	Proposed Course	Delivery Method	Course Length	Exists, Develop, or Buy	Budget
> Adjusters are not complying with DOI regulations.	Auto Adjusters, 860. Regional offices.	Auto Claims—Remaining in Compliance	WBT	1 hour	Develop in-house.	$12,000
	Homeowners Adjusters, 400. Regional offices.	Homeowners Claims—Remaining in Compliance	WBT	1 hour	Develop in-house.	$12,000
	Auto Claims Supervisors, 43. Homeowners Claims Supervisors, 20. Regional offices.	DOI File Review	WBT	2 hours	Develop in-house.	$17,000
> Improve customer service by reducing the time it takes to resolve a claim.	New Auto Adjusters, 460. Regional offices.	Investigating Auto Claims	Classroom	1 day	Outsource development.	$35,000
		Resolving Medical Payment Claims	Classroom	2 days	Outsource development.	$50,000
		Resolving Collision and Comprehensive Claims	Classroom	2 days	Outsource development.	$50,000
		Resolving BI, GBI, and PI Claims	Classroom	3 days	Outsource development.	$65,000
		Resolving Auto Property Damage Claims	Classroom	2 days	Outsource development.	$50,000

Training Plan and Budget

New Claims Division Training

Purpose or Link to Problem, Goal, or Issue	Training Audience	Proposed Course	Delivery Method	Course Length	Exists, Develop, or Buy	Budget
	New Homeowners Adjusters, 150. Regional offices.	Investigating Homeowners Claims	Classroom	1 day	Outsource development.	$35,000
		Resolving Dwelling and Other Structures Claims	Classroom	2 days	Outsource development.	$50,000
		Resolving Personal and Scheduled Property Claims	Classroom	2 days	Outsource development.	$50,000
		Resolving Medical Payment Claims	Classroom	2 days	Outsource development.	$50,000
		Resolving Homeowners Property Damage Claims	Classroom	2 days	Outsource development.	$50,000
	Claims Reporting Hotline Representatives, 1,000. Claims Reporting Center.	Introduction to Workload Balancing	CBT	1.5 hours	Develop in-house.	$18,000
	Claims Trainers, 12. Claims Reporting Center. Headquarters.	Train the Trainer (10 new courses)	Classroom	19 days	Develop in-house.	$27,000
					Total Budget for New Claims Training	$571,000

Appendix: Blank Templates

Template 1

Executive Interview Summary—Organizational Problems

Name > _____

Title > _____

Date > _____

Prioritize the problems based on how critical they are to organizational success.

Organizational Problems

High Priority >

_____

Medium Priority >

_____

Low Priority >

Template 2

Executive Interview Summary—Problem Worksheet

Name > _____

Title > _____

Date > _____

Complete a Problem Worksheet for each problem.

Problem > What is the problem?

_____

Operational Results > What operational results will indicate that the problem has been solved?

_____

Priority > Why is solving the problem critical to achieving organizational success?

Executive Interview Summary—Problem Worksheet

Division/Departments Involved in Solving the Problem	Actual Performance Today	Performance Required to Solve the Problem	Anticipated Learning Needs

Executive Interview Summary—Problem Worksheet

Factors Contributing to the Problem	Planned Changes to Address Factors	Divisions/Departments Impacted by Changes	Anticipated Learning Needs

Template 3

Executive Interview Summary—Organizational Goals

Name > _____

Title > _____

Date > _____

Prioritize the goals based on how critical they are to organizational success.

Organizational Goals

High Priority >

_____

Medium Priority >

_____

Low Priority >

Template 4

Executive Interview Summary—Goal Worksheet

Name > _____

Title > _____

Date > _____

Complete a Goal Worksheet for each goal.

Goal > What is the goal?

_____

Operational Results > What operational results will indicate the goal has been achieved?

_____

Priority > Why is achieving the goal critical to achieving organizational success?

Executive Interview Summary—Goal Worksheet

Division/Departments Involved in Achieving the Goal	Actual Performance Today	Performance Required to Achieve the Goal	Anticipated Learning Needs

Executive Interview Summary—Goal Worksheet

Barriers to Achieving the Goal	Planned Changes to Overcome Barriers	Divisions/Departments Impacted by Changes	Anticipated Learning Needs

Template 5

Division/Department Manager—Organizational Problems

Manager > _____

Division > _____

Date > _____

Prioritize the problems this division/department will be involved in solving based on how critical they are to organizational success.

Organizational Problems this Division/Department Will Be Involved in Solving

High Priority >

_____

Medium Priority >

_____

Low Priority >

Template 6

Division/Department Manager—Problem Summary

Manager > _____

Division > _____

Date > _____

Summarize the data for each problem identified by the executive team that this division/department will be involved in solving. Include only information that pertains to this division/department. Multiple divisions/departments may be involved in solving a particular problem. Review this information with the division/department manager at the start of the interview. In fact, you may want to send this form before the interview to help the manager prepare.

If the executive team did not identify this division/department as being involved in solving any organizational problems, skip the Problem Summary (Template 6) and Problem Worksheet (Template 7).

Problem > What is the problem?

_____

Operational Results > What operational results will indicate that the problem has been solved?

_____

Priority > Why is solving the problem critical to achieving organizational success?

_____

Performance Description > What will employees in this division/department need to do or do differently to solve this problem? How are these employees performing today? How will they need to perform to solve the problem?

Template 6 *(continued, p. 2)*

Division/Department Manager—Problem Summary

**Anticipated
Learning Needs >** What, if anything, will employees in this division/department need
to learn so they can solve the problem? (List only anticipated
learning needs for employees in this division/department.)

_____

Contributing Factors > Besides employee performance, what other factors contribute
to the problem?

_____

Planned Changes > What changes will be made to address these factors? (List only
changes that will impact this division/department.)

_____

**Anticipated
Learning Needs >** What, if anything, will employees in this division/department
need to learn as a result of these changes? (List only anticipated
learning needs for employees in this division/department.)

Template 7

Division/Department Manager—Problem Worksheet

Use the information you gather during your interview with the division/department manager to complete the Problem Worksheet. Include data from executive interviews plus new information this manager provides.

Positions Involved in Solving the Problem (Indicate title, number of employees, and location.)	Actual Performance Today	Performance Required to Solve the Problem	Anticipated Learning Needs

Template 7 (continued, p. 2)

Division/Department Manager—Problem Worksheet

Factors Contributing to the Problem	Planned Changes to Address Factors	Positions Impacted by Changes (Indicate title, number of employees, and location.)	Anticipated Learning Needs

Template 8
Division/Department Manager—Organizational Goals

Manager > _____

Division > _____

Date > _____

Prioritize the goals the division/department will be involved in achieving based on how critical they are to organizational success.

Organizational Goals this Division/Department Will Be Involved in Achieving

    High Priority >

    _____

    Medium Priority >

    _____

    Low Priority >

Template 9

Division/Department Manager—Goal Summary

Manager > _____

Division > _____

Date > _____

*Summarize the data for each goal identified by the executive team that this division/
department will be involved in achieving. Include only information that pertains to this
division/department. Multiple divisions/departments may be involved in achieving a particular goal. Review this information with the division/department manager at the start
of the interview. In fact, you may want to send this form before the interview to help the
manager prepare.*

*If the executive team did not identify this division/department as being involved in
achieving any organizational goals, skip the Goal Summary (Template 9) and Goal Worksheet (Template 10).*

Goal > What is the goal?

_____

Operational Results > What operational results will indicate that the goal has been
achieved?

_____

Priority > Why is achieving the goal critical to achieving organizational success?

_____

**Performance
Description >** What will employees in this division/department need to do or
do differently to achieve this goal? How are these employees performing today? How will they need to perform to achieve the goal?

Template 9 *(continued, p. 2)*

Division/Department Manager—Goal Summary

**Anticipated
Learning Needs** > What, if anything, will employees in this division/department
need to learn so they can solve the problem? (List only anticipated
learning needs for employees in this division/department.)

Contributing Factors > Besides employee performance, what other factors contribute to
the problem?

Planned Changes > What changes will be made to address these factors? (List only
changes that will impact this division/department.)

**Anticipated
Learning Needs** > What, if anything, will employees in this division/department
need to learn as a result of these changes? (List only anticipated
learning needs for employees in this division/department.)

Template 10
Division/Department Manager—Goal Worksheet

Use the information you gather during your interview with the division/department manager to complete the Goal Worksheet. Include data from executive interviews plus new information this manager provides.

Positions Involved in Achieving the Goal (Indicate title, number of employees, and location.)	Actual Performance Today	Performance Required to Achieve the Goal	Anticipated Learning Needs

Training Budgets Step-by-Step. Copyright © 2004 by John Wiley & Sons, Inc. Reproduced by permission of Pfeiffer, an Imprint of Wiley. www.pfeiffer.com

Division/Department Manager—Goal Worksheet

Barriers to Achieving the Goal	Planned Changes to Overcome Barriers	Positions Impacted by Changes (Indicate title, number of employees, and location.)	Anticipated Learning Needs

Training Budgets Step-by-Step. Copyright © 2004 by John Wiley & Sons, Inc. Reproduced by permission of Pfeiffer, an Imprint of Wiley. www.pfeiffer.com

Template 11

Division/Department Manager—Issues

Manager > _____

Division > _____

Date > _____

Prioritize the issues identified by this division/department manager based on how critical they are to organizational success.

Division/Department Issues

High Priority >

_____

Medium Priority >

_____

Low Priority >

Template 12

Division/Department Manager—Issue Worksheet

Complete an Issue Worksheet for each issue identified by this manager.

Issue > What is the issue?

_____

Cause > What is the cause of the issue?

_____

Result > What is the result of this issue? What difficulty is this issue causing?

_____

Operational Results > What operational results will indicate that the issue has been resolved?

_____

Link to Problem or a Goal > Can this issue be linked to a problem or goal the executive team identified? If so, how?

Template 12 *(continued, p. 2)*

Division/Department Manager—Issue Worksheet

Positions Involved in Resolving the Issue (Indicate title, number of employees, and location.)	Actual Performance Today	Performance Required to Resolve the Issue	Anticipated Learning Needs

Division/Department Manager—Issue Worksheet

Barriers to Resolving the Issue	Planned Changes to Overcome Barriers	Positions Impacted by Changes (Indicate title, number of employees, and location.)	Anticipated Learning Needs

Template 13

Existing Training Worksheet

Add to this Existing Training Worksheet as you interview each person. Don't forget to include courses that don't fall under any particular division/department, such as New Employee Orientation. Ultimately, this worksheet should contain a comprehensive list of existing training that is being offered throughout the organization.

Course Title	Training Audience (Indicate title, number of employees, and location.)	Mandatory? (Yes or No)	Delivery Method (classroom, WBT, etc.)	Course Length	Cost/Session	Number of Sessions per Year	Up-to-Date? (Yes or No)	Notes

Template 14

Training Plan and Budget

Purpose or Link to Problem, Goal, or Issue	Training Audience	Proposed Course	Delivery Method	Course Length	Exists, Develop, or Buy	Budget

Template 15
New Courses Worksheet

Use the worksheet below to turn learning needs into possible courses.

Problem, Goal, or Issue	Learning Needs	Course	Mandatory? (Yes or No)	Training Audience

Training Budgets Step-by-Step. Copyright © 2004 by John Wiley & Sons, Inc. Reproduced by permission of Pfeiffer, an Imprint of Wiley. www.pfeiffer.com

About the Author

DIANE VALENTI, president of Applied Learning Solutions, Inc., has fifteen years' experience in instructional design. She specializes in creating systems, job-specific processes and procedures, and new product training for Fortune 1000 companies.

Ms. Valenti is currently teaching in the extension program at UC Berkeley. She has been featured in articles in *Training & Development* and *Training* magazine on using games in training and in ASTD's e-zine, *Learning Circuits*.

She holds a master's degree in education and human development from the George Washington University in Washington, D.C. And, she recently earned her certification in project management from the Project Management Institute.

Index

Contents of the CD-ROM

Delivery Setting

Delivery Approach

Appendix: Blank Templates

Template 9: Division/Department Manager—Goal Summary

Template 10: Division/Department Manager—Goal Worksheet

Template 11: Division/Department Manager—Issues

Template 12: Division/Department Manager—Issue Worksheet

Template 13: Existing Training Worksheet

Template 14: Training Plan and Budget

Template 15: New Courses Worksheet

How to Use the CD-ROM

System Requirements

Windows PC

- 486 or Pentium processor-based personal computer

- Microsoft Windows 95 or Windows NT 3.51 or later

- Minimum RAM: 8 MB for Windows 95 and NT

- Available space on hard disk: 8 MB Windows 95 and NT

- 2X speed CD-ROM drive or faster

- Netscape 4.0 or higher browser or MS Internet Explorer 4.0 or higher

- Microsoft Word 97 or higher

Macintosh

- Macintosh with a 68020 or higher processor or Power Macintosh

- Apple OS version 7.0 or later

- Minimum RAM: 12 MB for Macintosh

- Available space on hard disk: 6MB Macintosh

- 2X speed CD-ROM drive or faster

- Netscape 4.0 or higher browser or MS Internet Explorer 4.0 or higher

- Microsoft Word 98 or higher

NOTE: This CD also requires the free Acrobat Reader. You can download these products using the links below:
http://www.netscape.com/download/index.html
http://www.adobe.com/products/acrobat/readstep.html

Getting Started

Insert the CD-ROM into your drive. The CD-ROM will usually launch automatically. If it does not, click on the CD-ROM drive on your computer to launch. You will see an opening page. You can click on this page or wait for it to fade to the Copyright Page. After you click to agree to the terms of the Copyright Page, the Home Page will appear.

Moving Around

Use the buttons at the left of each screen or the text at the bottom of each screen to move among the menu pages. To view a document listed on one of the menu pages, simply click on the name of the document. Use the scroll-bar at the right of the screen to scroll up and down each page. To quit a document at any time, click the box at the upper right-hand corner of the screen. To quit the CD-ROM, you can click the Quit button on the left of each menu page or hit Control-Q if you are a PC user or Command-Q if you are a Mac user.

In Case Of Trouble

If you experience difficulty using this CD-ROM, please follow these steps:

1. Make sure your hardware and systems configurations conform to the systems requirements noted under "Systems Requirements" above.

2. Review the installation procedure for your type of hardware and operating system. It is possible to reinstall the software if necessary.

   You may call Pfeiffer Customer Care at (800) 274–4434 between the hours of 8 A. M. and 4 P. M. Eastern Standard Time, and ask for Pfeiffer Product Technical Support. You can also get support information and contact Product Technical Support through our website at http://www.wiley.com/techsupport.

3. Please have the following information available:

   • Type of computer and operating system

   • Version of Windows or Mac OS being used

   • Any error messages displayed

   • Complete description of the problem.

   (It is best if you are sitting at your computer when making the call.)

Pfeiffer Publications Guide

This guide is designed to familiarize you with the various types of Pfeiffer publications. The formats section describes the various types of products that we publish; the methodologies section describes the many different ways that content might be provided within a product. We also provide a list of the topic areas in which we publish.

FORMATS

In addition to its extensive book-publishing program, Pfeiffer offers content in an array of formats, from fieldbooks for the practitioner to complete, ready-to-use training packages that support group learning.

FIELDBOOK Designed to provide information and guidance to practitioners in the midst of action. Most fieldbooks are companions to another, sometimes earlier, work, from which its ideas are derived; the fieldbook makes practical what was theoretical in the original text. Fieldbooks can certainly be read from cover to cover. More likely, though, you'll find yourself bouncing around following a particular theme, or dipping in as the mood, and the situation, dictate.

HANDBOOK A contributed volume of work on a single topic, comprising an eclectic mix of ideas, case studies, and best practices sourced by practitioners and experts in the field.

An editor or team of editors usually is appointed to seek out contributors and to evaluate content for relevance to the topic. Think of a handbook not as a ready-to-eat meal, but as a cookbook of ingredients that enables you to create the most fitting experience for the occasion.

RESOURCE Materials designed to support group learning. They come in many forms: a complete, ready-to-use exercise (such as a game); a comprehensive resource on one topic (such as conflict management) containing a variety of methods and approaches; or a collection of like-minded activities (such as icebreakers) on multiple subjects and situations.

TRAINING PACKAGE An entire, ready-to-use learning program that focuses on a particular topic or skill. All packages comprise a guide for the facilitator/trainer and a workbook for the participants. Some packages are supported with additional media—such as video—or learning aids, instruments, or other devices to help participants understand concepts or practice and develop skills.

- *Facilitator/trainer's guide* Contains an introduction to the program, advice on how to organize and facilitate the learning event, and step-by-step instructor notes. The guide also contains copies of presentation materials—handouts, presentations, and overhead designs, for example—used in the program.

- *Participant's workbook* Contains exercises and reading materials that support the learning goal and serve as a valuable reference and support guide for participants in the weeks and months that follow the learning event. Typically, each participant will require his or her own workbook.

ELECTRONIC CD-ROMs and web-based products transform static Pfeiffer content into dynamic, interactive experiences. Designed to take advantage of the searchability, automation, and ease-of-use that technology provides, our e-products bring convenience and immediate accessibility to your workspace.

METHODOLOGIES

CASE STUDY A presentation, in narrative form, of an actual event that has occurred inside an organization. Case studies are not prescriptive, nor are they used to prove a point; they are designed to develop critical analysis and decision-making skills. A case study has a specific time frame, specifies a sequence of events, is narrative in structure, and contains a plot structure— an issue (what should be/have been done?). Use case studies when the goal is to enable participants to apply previously learned theories to the circumstances in the case, decide what is pertinent, identify the real issues, decide what should have been done, and develop a plan of action.

ENERGIZER A short activity that develops readiness for the next session or learning event. Energizers are most commonly used after a break or lunch to stimulate or refocus the group. Many involve some form of physical activity, so they are a useful way to counter post-lunch lethargy. Other uses include transitioning from one topic to another, where "mental" distancing is important.

EXPERIENTIAL LEARNING ACTIVITY (ELA) A facilitator-led intervention that moves participants through the learning cycle from experience to application (also known as a Structured Experience). ELAs are carefully thought-out designs in which there is a definite learning purpose and intended outcome. Each step—everything that participants do during the activity— facilitates the accomplishment of the stated goal. Each ELA includes complete instructions for facilitating the intervention and a clear statement of goals, suggested group size and timing, materials required, an explanation of the process, and, where appropriate, possible variations to the activity. (For more detail on Experiential Learning Activities, see the Introduction to the *Reference Guide to Handbooks and Annuals*, 1999 edition, Pfeiffer, San Francisco.)

GAME A group activity that has the purpose of fostering team spirit and togetherness in addition to the achievement of a pre-stated goal. Usually contrived—undertaking a desert expedition, for example—this type of learning method offers an engaging means for participants to demonstrate and practice business and interpersonal skills. Games are effective for team building and personal development mainly because the goal is subordinate to the process—the means through which participants reach decisions, collaborate, communicate, and generate trust and understanding. Games often engage teams in "friendly" competition.

ICEBREAKER A (usually) short activity designed to help participants overcome initial anxiety in a training session and/or to acquaint the participants with one another. An icebreaker can be a fun activity or can be tied to specific topics or training goals. While a useful tool in itself, the icebreaker comes into its own in situations where tension or resistance exists within a group.

INSTRUMENT A device used to assess, appraise, evaluate, describe, classify, and summarize various aspects of human behavior. The term used to describe an instrument depends primarily on its format and purpose. These terms include survey, questionnaire, inventory, diagnostic survey, and poll. Some uses of instruments include providing instrumental feedback to group members, studying here-and-now processes or functioning within a group, manipulating group composition, and evaluating outcomes of training and other interventions.

Instruments are popular in the training and HR field because, in general, more growth can occur if an individual is provided with a method for focusing specifically on his or her own behavior. Instruments also are used to obtain information that will serve as a basis for change and to assist in workforce planning efforts.

Paper-and-pencil tests still dominate the instrument landscape with a typical package comprising a facilitator's guide, which offers advice on administering the instrument and interpreting the collected data, and an initial set of instruments. Additional instruments are available separately. Pfeiffer, though, is investing heavily in e-instruments. Electronic instrumentation provides effortless distribution and, for larger groups particularly, offers advantages over paper-and-pencil tests in the time it takes to analyze data and provide feedback.

LECTURETTE A short talk that provides an explanation of a principle, model, or process that is pertinent to the participants' current learning needs. A lecturette is intended to establish a common language bond between the trainer and the participants by providing a mutual frame of reference. Use a lecturette as an introduction to a group activity or event, as an interjection during an event, or as a handout.

MODEL A graphic depiction of a system or process and the relationship among its elements. Models provide a frame of reference and something more tangible, and more easily remembered, than a verbal explanation. They also give participants something to "go on," enabling them to track their own progress as they experience the dynamics, processes, and relationships being depicted in the model.

ROLE PLAY A technique in which people assume a role in a situation/scenario: a customer service rep in an angry-customer exchange, for example. The way in which the role is approached is then discussed and feedback is offered. The role play is often repeated using a different approach and/or incorporating changes made based on feedback received. In other words, role playing is a spontaneous interaction involving realistic behavior under artificial (and safe) conditions.

SIMULATION A methodology for understanding the interrelationships among components of a system or process. Simulations differ from games in that they test or use a model that depicts or mirrors some aspect of reality in form, if not necessarily in content. Learning occurs by studying the effects of change on one or more factors of the model. Simulations are commonly used to test hypotheses about what happens in a system—often referred to as "what if?" analysis—or to examine best-case/worst-case scenarios.

THEORY A presentation of an idea from a conjectural perspective. Theories are useful because they encourage us to examine behavior and phenomena through a different lens.

TOPICS

The twin goals of providing effective and practical solutions for workforce training and organization development and meeting the educational needs of training and human resource professionals shape Pfeiffer's publishing program. Core topics include the following:

Leadership & Management

Communication & Presentation

Coaching & Mentoring

Training & Development

e-Learning

Teams & Collaboration

OD & Strategic Planning

Human Resources

Consulting

Customer Care

Have a question, comment, or suggestion? Contact us! We value your feedback and we want to hear from you.

For questions about this or other Pfeiffer products, you may contact us by:

E-mail: **customer@wiley.com**

Mail: **Customer Care Wiley/Pfeiffer**
10475 Crosspoint Blvd.
Indianapolis, IN 46256

Phone: **(US) 800-274-4434** (Outside the US: 317-572-3985)

Fax: **(US) 800-569-0443** (Outside the US: 317-572-4002)

To order additional copies of this title or to browse other Pfeiffer products, visit us online at **www.pfeiffer.com**.

For **Technical Support** questions call **(800) 274-4434.**

For authors guidelines, log on to www.pfeiffer.com and click on "Resources for Authors."

If you are . . .

A **college bookstore, a professor, an instructor, or work in higher education** and you'd like to place an order or request an exam copy, please contact jbreview@wiley.com.

A **general retail bookseller** and you'd like to establish an account or speak to a local sales representative, contact Melissa Grecco at 201-748-6267 or mgrecco@wiley.com.

An **exclusively on-line bookseller**, contact Amy Blanchard at 530-756-9456 or ablanchard @wiley.com or Jennifer Johnson at 206-568-3883 or jjohnson@wiley.com, both of our Online Sales department.

A **librarian or library representative**, contact John Chambers in our Library Sales department at 201-748-6291 or jchamber@wiley.com.

A **reseller, training company/consultant, or corporate trainer**, contact Charles Regan in our Special Sales department at 201-748-6553 or cregan@wiley.com.

A **specialty retail distributor** (includes specialty gift stores, museum shops, and corporate bulk sales), contact Kim Hendrickson in our Special Sales department at 201-748-6037 or khendric@wiley.com.

Purchasing for the **Federal government**, contact Ron Cunningham in our Special Sales department at 317-572-3053 or rcunning@wiley.com.

Purchasing for a **State or Local government**, contact Charles Regan in our Special Sales department at 201-748-6553 or cregan@wiley.com.

What will you find on pfeiffer.com?

- The best in workplace performance solutions for training and HR professionals

- Downloadable training tools, exercises, and content

- Web-exclusive offers

- Training tips, articles, and news

- Seamless on-line ordering

- Author guidelines, information on becoming a Pfeiffer Affiliate, and much more

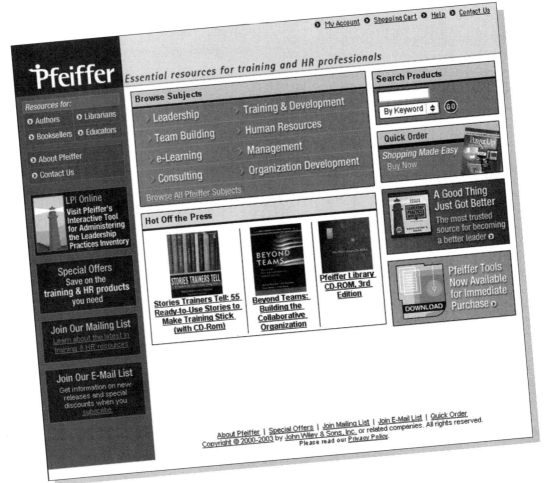

Discover more at www.pfeiffer.com